THIRD EDITION

Understand
your
Accounts

A Guide to Small Business Finance

A ST JOHN PRICE

**KOGAN
PAGE**

First published in 1978 by Lynxplan (Sheffield) Limited
Revised edition published in 1979 by Kogan Page Limited,
   reprinted 1981
Second edition 1986
Third edition 1991

Kogan Page Limited
120 Pentonville Road
London N1 9JN

© A St J Price 1978, 1979, 1986, 1991

British Library Cataloguing in Publication Data

A CIP record for this book is available from the British Library.

ISBN 0-7494-0368-3

Typeset by BookEns Limited, Baldock, Herts.
Printed and bound in Great Britain by
Clays Ltd, St Ives plc

Contents

Introduction

If your annual accounts are a mystery to you;
If you don't understand budgets, let alone a cash flow forecast;
If your finances are a constant worry – especially the cash position;
If you don't understand your accountant – and vice versa;
If you feel you don't get the help you need from your accountant;
If you're not even sure what help you ought to get in return for the fees you pay;
If you think that better financial control might improve your profits – but aren't sure how to start – this is the book for you.

I strip away the mystery from figures and show you how to use them as a key tool in running your business. I explain how to read a balance sheet and unlock the vital information your accounts contain.

Have you ever had the feeling that your accountant, whether internal or external, is sitting on information you need and could have – if only you understood enough of the jargon to get it out of him or her? I know that feeling from the other side. I have been the financial director of a business where I had to get through to my colleagues if we were not to go bust. Later, I ran courses on finance for non-accountants and learnt the hard way how to explain figures to experienced executives, who were quick to challenge any jargon they did not understand.

So this book condenses my knowledge, born of hard experience, into simple, clear explanations. I give detailed examples and take you through them line by line. One cannot avoid the jargon of accounting if one is to understand accounts but my methods of explaining have been tested on audiences ranging from housewives to company directors. And, once you've got the idea, oh joy, you'll never again be lost in a fog of words instead of getting what you want from your accountant!

Do I exaggerate? Well, when I showed one managing director the cash flow report described in Chapter 13 – *How to Get a Grip on Your Cash Position – Now* – he exclaimed that he had wanted such a report for years but that his accountant had always maintained it was not possible. Yet the figures were readily available in his accounting system once he knew where to look.

At the end of the book, in Part 3, there's a worked example of how to produce a complete budget for a small business, step by step. I show you how to save time while making sure that your budget is the valuable business tool it ought to be.

This is a concise guide to what really matters in business finance. Even if you work for a big organisation, you need to understand those principles. It is not a tome on financial management. If you want a thesis on elaborate controls for the larger business, there are plenty of others – but they will take you a lot longer to read!

To get an idea of whether my book delivers on those promises, I suggest you glance through Chapter 1 – *Why You Need Financial Controls in Your Business*, Chapters 4 and 5 on the profit and loss account and the balance sheet, and the 'tank chart' in Chapter 11, *How Cash Circulates in a Business*.

How to use this book

If you get stuck on a point, leave it and carry on. Read the whole book once and then go back over the points of difficulty or special interest more slowly. Do not worry if parts seem difficult at first. The earlier chapters end with questions to help you test your understanding.

A St J Price, FCA
Cirencester
January 1991

Chapter 1

Why You Need Financial Controls in Your Business

Business is a high risk activity: long-term success does not usually come easily. Many people fail because it is tough, not because they deserve to lose. Enthusiasm, hard work, intelligence – these attributes do not guarantee survival. Only generating cash will do that. Financial control adequate to ensure that there's cash to pay the bills is usually the ingredient whose absence leads to business failure.

You don't *have* to have good financial control to win in business – but without it your chances are much lower. In fact you are gambling, not managing.

So financial control is about maximising your chances of survival and making sure that no one disaster can sink you. It enables you to grab the opportunities and maximise your good luck while avoiding some of the bad luck and minimising the rest.

Why financial control will maximise your chances of survival

You can't run a business without money. Whatever other reasons you may have for being in business, making money is vital. Without it your business will fail.

To survive in the short term you have to be able to pay the bills. That means making sure that your activities result in enough cash in the bank to meet your liabilities as they become due. It takes a good grip on the financial aspects of a business to make sure the money is available when needed.

To succeed in the long term, you must make a profit as well. While it's cash that pays the bills, it's profits which will keep you in business. Over the longer term, you must make sufficient profit to be able to finance the growth of the business and to invest in the equipment, premises or whatever is needed to ensure its future prosperity.

Profit and cash are not the same. It's all too common for a business to make a profit without enough cash coming in to keep it going. Profit tends to get tied up in stocks, debtors,

15

equipment etc. If this results in a shortage of cash to pay the bills, you cannot trade properly but must waste time and energy fending off your creditors. Once such crises begin, they tend to become worse and worse until, eventually, you may have to close down or sell out. Why that happens and what jargon like 'stocks' and debtors' means will be explained later.

For now, the key point is that profits will only keep the business going if they produce enough cash, and they will only do that if you have good financial control. In contrast, a concern making losses but which has reserves of cash can survive for as long as good financial control enables it to eke out that cash. Therefore it is just as important to plan for cash as it is for profit.

What is financial control?

Full financial control means:

- Knowing where you are now – annual accounts
- Planning where you are going – budgets
- Making sure you get there   – progress reports and controls to check what's going on.

You cannot achieve all this at once. To begin, you need an understanding of what your annual accounts tell you about the business so that's where this book starts. Though the second stage is shown above as producing a budget, I deal first with some simple controls and progress reports. The reason is that you must have reliable and prompt information about the key facts of your current financial position before you can budget realistically. Even more to the point, you can do something about installing these controls and reports straight away – in fact they are in one sense more important than a budget because, until you have today under control, plans for tomorrow are likely to stay wishful thinking. Budgets are based upon the understanding that the first two parts of the book will give you.

Your accounts are a goldmine of facts

Your accounts contain valuable clues about the state of your business but poor presentation may make them difficult to unearth. Accounts do not talk – you must read them. Your records must first be organised so that they produce the right figures; then those figures must be interpreted and made to tell the story. To understand that story, not only do you need to be able to read a set of accounts but also to understand how the numbers relate to each other. That's what you'll be shown in the next few chapters: where to look for the gold which is hidden under all that accountant's jargon.

The jargon will be explained, but I won't try to turn you into an accountant – just equip you with enough knowledge to understand your figures.

Why your accountant does not do this for you

Have you ever wished your accountant would do just what I am promising – and wondered why it did not happen? Well, it's your money, isn't it? (Even if you only run a part of someone else's business, they are your figures on which you are judged.) The interest must begin with *you*. Your accountant, whether an external auditor or an internal colleague, is a busy person. With many demands on his (or her) time, he'll naturally do most for the client or colleague who takes an informed interest in the figures he produces. Such a client is much easier to help than the one who has to be prodded into even looking at the numbers. Besides, the key to getting the best answers from any specialist is knowing the questions to ask.

That's the rub! You aren't sure of the questions or you would not be reading this, and most accountants are not very good at explaining finance to laymen anyway. To do so clearly is a skill requiring practice they often have not had. Most non-accountants have trouble with the financial aspects of business unless they are lucky enough to have at their elbow one of those rare accountants who are good at explaining the results of their labours. If finance troubles you too, this book will help you.

Chapter 2

The Ownership of a Business

If you know the difference between a sole trader, a partner and a director of a limited company just skim this section quickly to check for any points new to you. If you don't know, the following explanation will help you understand some of the later chapters.

A business can operate as a sole trader, a partnership, a limited company or as a cooperative. There are important legal and tax differences and each has advantages and disadvantages.

What is a sole trader?

A sole trader is an individual who works for himself though not necessarily alone; he may have employees. All the profits (or losses) are his and he pays income tax on them as an individual, though of course under the rules for business profits, not under Pay As You Earn (PAYE).

He may trade under his own name or one which describes it, such as Acme Window Cleaners. Sometimes, when a business is sold, the new owner retains the name of the previous owner.

What is a partnership?

A partnership is a group of two or more people who agree to share the risks, profits and losses of a business. They can agree whatever terms they wish as to who contributes what money or time to the business and how the profits are shared. Each partner, however, is responsible for all the debts incurred by the business. Each can therefore be made bankrupt should a creditor decide to claim from him because he has assets and his partners do not, or even perhaps because they have disappeared. Thus a partnership has no *legal* existence in its own right – it is just a group of individuals who agree to work together sharing not just premises, equipment etc, but also the profits or losses resulting from their activities.

The partnership agreement can be verbal but it is much more sensible to put it in writing. A partnership can also trade under a different name from those of the partners. Each partner is taxed individually on his or her share of the partnership profits, as shown by the partnership accounts, under the income tax rules.

What is a limited company?

A limited company is a separate legal entity in its own right. It is governed by strict rules in the Companies Acts and it can only be set up after complying with various formalities.

It must file accounts with the Registrar of Companies each year which are open to public inspection. It is illegal to add the word 'Limited' to your trading name until your company has complied with the Registrar's requirements and he has issued a certificate of registration.

The reason for this formality is that 'limited' means limited liability for the shareholders. They can lose only the money that they have put into the company. This is in contrast with sole traders or partners who must use their private assets if necessary to meet the debts of their businesses and who can be made bankrupt for those debts.

Since a limited company is a legal entity in its own right, it can make contracts and can sue or be sued. Naturally the people running the company act on its behalf, but they cannot usually be held personally responsible for the results unless, of course, they have given personal guarantees. There are exceptions: a director can be held responsible for unpaid National Insurance (NI) contributions, for instance, and must not act recklessly or illegally.

A limited company pays corporation tax on its profits. It deducts PAYE from the pay of its employees, including the salaries of directors, and must pass that deduction on to the government like any other employer. The profits of a limited company belong to the shareholders, as explained below.

A 'public limited company' (abbreviated to PLC) is a larger version of a 'limited' company. For instance, all companies whose shares are quoted on a stock exchange are PLCs. An unquoted company can also be a PLC. The differences are a matter of company law and need not concern us here.

What is a cooperative?

A cooperative is an association of people who join together to achieve mutually agreed aims. They have equal standing in the business. The members are the shareholders. The cooperative may be set up as a partnership or a limited company, in which case the above comments apply. Cooperatives registered as cooperative societies are registered under the Industrial and Provident Societies Acts 1965–78 and the law is administered by the Registrar of Friendly Societies. They pay corporation tax and must file audited accounts annually with their Registrar.

A company goes on for ever

Unlike a sole trader, who can cease trading at will, or a partnership which can be dissolved, a company continues indefinitely. It only ceases to have a legal existence if its shareholders decide to close it down or if its creditors force it into liquidation because it has not paid their bills.

When the majority shareholder of a company dies, the company carries on, whereas if a sole trader dies, his business ceases in law and the assets pass to his heirs who begin a new business even if they continue trading the way he did. Of course, in the case of a one-man company there is little practical difference but the heirs inherit the shares in the company, not the actual assets of the business.

What are 'shareholders' and 'directors'?

The *shareholders* own the company. When the company is formed, they subscribe for shares in it (called share capital), paying for them either in cash or in assets. For instance, when a sole trader incorporates his business as a limited company, he receives shares in exchange for the equipment, goods etc handed over to the company. Share capital is explained in more detail in Chapter 6.

The *board of directors* runs the business. Individual directors may or may not own shares in it but, in small businesses, the directors and shareholders are often the same people. The directors of a small company usually work full time in it.

In large companies, some of the directors may be 'non-executive'. These are not managers working full time in the business;

they merely attend board meetings. They are really consultants or advisers and their fees are often much smaller than the salaries of the full-time directors.

Who controls the company – directors or shareholders?

In companies where they are not the same people, it is the directors who run the business. They are responsible for preparing the accounts which they must present to the shareholders each year for approval at the annual general meeting. There are also certain actions for which they have to obtain the approval of the shareholders, such as increases in the share capital.

Theoretically the shareholders of a major company can tell the directors what to do. Usually it is not practical for them to run the business of the company themselves – there may be many thousands of them for one thing – so this really means that they can vote new directors on to the board, who they think will run the business more to their liking than the old ones.

In large companies the directors often hold a very small proportion of the shares. In practice they are not often voted out by the shareholders unless they have run the business very badly or unless their conduct has been highly controversial and public opinion has been aroused.

Salaries for directors and dividends for shareholders

Directors are paid salaries or fees with deduction of PAYE and NI contributions, just like any other employee.

Shareholders receive dividends on their shares, if there are enough profits to pay them and if they decide to take a dividend. In small companies where they are the same people, directors often pay themselves salaries rather than take dividends. Earned income in the past had tax advantages compared with an unearned dividend. The 1984 Finance Act changed the rules and the removal of the ceiling for employers' NI contributions in 1985 increased the company's tax bill for high salaries, so dividends now have advantages – until the rules alter again!

Why trade as a limited company?

Many small companies are really only sole traders who have chosen to trade under limited liability. The practical trading differences, as opposed to legal ones, are few in such cases. Moreover, the advantages to the owner of limited liability for the debts of his business are often less than they seem at first sight.

Banks often demand security or personal guarantees, or both, from the directors to cover an overdraft, while the Department of Social Security can sue them for National Insurance contributions if the company fails to pay them over. In practice, therefore, the owners of a small business often obtain protection only from their suppliers, useful though that can be.

Limited liability can be helpful in trades which have a high failure rate, such as builders, or a high potential public liability, such as food or drug manufacturers.

Being in business is never without risk and limited liability allows large businesses to function without the directors being personally involved in any losses. As explained below, it also allows outsiders to invest money in the business without having to manage it. Without the rules of limited liability, it would be impossible for big businesses to exist because the necessary finances can only be provided by outside shareholders. The directors could not do so on their own.

There can also be tax advantages in having a company. However, the profit figure at which that becomes true is often higher than is supposed. The position changes from time to time as governments alter the tax rules so advice from a good accountant is essential.

If a business grows too big for one man or a small number of partners to manage, incorporation also enables them to allow their employees a stake in the business by issuing shares to them. It can also be easier to pass on a limited company to the founder's children in the same way by giving them shares during his lifetime.

For many small businesses, however, there is not much advantage in becoming a limited company. There can be serious tax disadvantages if the owner(s) wish to take out cash which has accumulated in the company. Moreover, if partners incorporate their business but then fall out, the company cannot simply be divided up like the assets of a partnership. It has a legal existence of its own and dissolving it or buying out one of its shareholders can cause legal and tax problems, especially if relationships are bad.

Another serious disadvantage of a limited company is that it is subject to more red tape. It has to file accounts each year with the Registrar of Companies. Moreover, the layout of those accounts and the information shown in them are tightly regulated by the Companies Acts, supplemented by rules laid down by the professional accounting bodies. There are complex requirements designed to protect shareholders and creditors which are often meaningless for the small family-controlled company. They also cause high audit fees.

Whereas a sole trader or partnership needs accounts primarily to help run the business and to keep the tax man quiet, a company must have its accounts audited by a qualified professional accountant who must certify that they comply with the requirements; if they do not, he must say so and why. This means extra time complying with the rules even though the resulting information usually means nothing to the owner of a small company.

A good professional accountant is invaluable to the small business because of the advice he can offer but the extra cost of an audit certificate in the case of a company is bad news.

Do not confuse '& Co' with a limited company

The word 'company' is often loosely used in business. 'J Bloggs & Co' sounds more imposing than 'J Bloggs'. Sole traders or partnerships can add the words '& Co' to their trading names if they wish and this has no legal effect. However, when people talk of 'a company', they usually mean a 'limited' company as described above.

Can a small company raise money by issuing shares?

There is no reason why a small company should not issue shares to outsiders, but it is illegal to issue a prospectus to the public at large asking them to subscribe for shares, unless you first comply with certain rules.

However, the taxation rules have been altered to make it more attractive for investors to put money into the smaller company through the Business Expansion Scheme. This has resulted in a number of financial organisations promoting funds which accept money from investors for placing under the scheme. Whether these will succeed in making enough profits on their successes to cover the inevitable losses remains to be seen. The issue of shares to outsiders is not a practical proposition for most small businesses, if only because most of the owners dislike sharing the ownership of their business.

Summary

A business can be owned by either a sole trader, a partnership, a limited company or a cooperative (which can function as a partnership or a limited company). Sole traders are taxed on their profits under income tax as are partners on their share of the partnership profits. A company's profits are taxed under corporation tax though small companies run by their owners often pay out most of the profit as salaries to the directors. The profit is then subject to income tax in the hands of each director under the PAYE rules rather than left in the company to pay corporation tax.

Companies have to file accounts for public inspection whereas sole traders and partnerships do not. Moreover, the form these accounts take is strictly controlled and they are in consequence more expensive to produce.

The example of a set of accounts in Chapter 3 is for the sole trader – as the simplest situation. Later on we shall see what the accounts of a limited company look like – though I stress that this book is about accounts for use in managing your business. Little time is spent on details which are only there because the law says they must be, however small the company.

What Do Annual Accounts Consist of?

Annual accounts consist of a *profit and loss account* and a *balance sheet*. The profit and loss account shows what has happened during the year and whether the result is a profit or a loss; the balance sheet shows where the business has then got to, ie what it owns and what it owes – its assets and its liabilities.

These accounts state in formal terms what you no doubt do informally in managing your personal affairs. During the month you earn so much in salary, or draw so much from your business, and spend this on food, rent or mortgage, clothes, entertainment, beer etc. At the end of the month you add up what you have left. You may have some money left over; perhaps you have no cash left or you owe some to other people or to your bank. The point is that you need to know whether you have spent more or less money than you have earned in that month. This is your personal profit and loss account – a statement of what has happened during the month.

In summing up your affairs, you will take into account any exceptional spending on furniture or video equipment, for example, things that will be of use to you for some time ahead. You could even draw up a personal balance sheet. Most of your spending would have no further value to you, but things such as furniture, clothes and so on could be listed and a figure put on them. You could thus show whether your net worth in terms of things owned and money in the bank was greater or less at the end of the month than at the beginning.

The profit and loss account

You may also meet the terms 'trading account' and 'appropriation account' which are jargon for sections of the profit and loss account.

The profit and loss account shows the profit or loss made during the period covered (a month, quarter, year etc). This is after allowing for bills owed but not yet paid (creditors), amounts owed to the business but not yet received (debtors) and sums, such as rent, paid for periods not yet finished (payments in advance).

The balance sheet

The balance sheet shows the value of the business at the date to which the profit and loss account was made up. It lists the assets: buildings, equipment, stocks, debtors, cash etc – and the liabilities: loans, creditors, bank overdraft and so on. The difference between the two totals is the owners's interest in the business. If it is a limited company this is called share capital and reserves; if it is a partnership or a sole trader it is shown as partner's or owner's capital and current accounts.

The owner's interest is in fact the original cash put into the business, plus profits earned since after tax, less cash drawn out.

The next two chapters explain the profit and loss account and the balance sheet in detail, define the accounting jargon and show you which are the key figures and ratios. You do not have to learn all the accountancy language but you do need enough understanding of the more important terms to be able to read your accounts and discuss them with your accountant.

Who sees the accounts (apart from the owners or shareholders)?

Every business needs accounts in order to agree its tax liability. In addition, a limited company must file a copy of its accounts with the Registrar of Companies, and a cooperative with the Registrar of Friendly Societies, where they are available for public inspection.

The bank manager may ask to see a copy, particularly if he has lent money to the business. The VAT inspector also has the right to ask to see the accounts.

How often are accounts needed?

Normally accounts are prepared annually but this may vary. Progressive businessmen use their accounts to help them run their business. It is often helpful to have half-yearly, quarterly or even monthly accounts in order to provide up-to-date information on the business.

How frequently you need them depends on your business. In many cases, the small businessman does not need complete figures during the year. Provided he has an overall grasp of his annual results and he has projected a budget for the coming year, he can keep track of what is happening by comparing the key figures against his forecast. There are usually only two or three key figures, which alter from month to month, such as sales, purchase of goods for resale, and wages. Often he can keep an eye on these during the year without formal accounts.

That really only applies to the smallest businesses, however, and even they can benefit from, say, quarterly accounts. Without them, it is so easy for things to go wrong financially without your noticing. Producing regular accounts forces you to add up and make sense of the numbers. That often highlights horror stories before they have gone on long enough for the loss to be serious.

Questions

Check your answers with the text.

- What is the difference between a profit and loss account and a balance sheet?
- Does the profit and loss account show:
  (a) the value of expenses incurred (ie commitments made), or
  (b) those actually spent (cash paid out)?

Chapter 4

The Profit and Loss Account Explained

As mentioned in Chapter 3 the profit and loss account shows how much profit (or loss) you have made. The example on page 29 is of an account for a small shop. It starts with sales, deducts the cost of sales to show the gross profit, then deducts expenses to show the net profit (or loss). Each of these headings is explained below. Please read the notes in conjunction with the example.

'Last year' and 'this year'

The figures for last year are given to show how the results for this year (the year just ended) have changed. Often a comparison with the figure for last year is more useful in helping you to understand the progress of your business than looking at this year in isolation. Changes in figures reveal trends which can be compared with what you think ought to have happened, perhaps showing you where action is needed to correct a problem. If you cannot rationalise a change, something is probably wrong. That applies when a figure is better than you expected, ie income is higher or a cost is lower. Investigation could reveal a mistake – sometimes simple errors such as adding up incorrectly or putting an amount under the wrong heading are highlighted by comparisons with the previous period. Comparisons are one of the most useful techniques in looking at figures.

Sales (or takings or turnover) £475,000

This is the value of goods sold (or services provided in, say, a hairdressing salon or a contracting business). It does not include VAT because that belongs to the government. It is net of any credits to customers for returns, discounts etc, though these could be shown as a separate deduction if significant.

If you sell on credit, you count as sales the value of goods

THE XYZ SHOP
Profit and loss account for the year ended 30 June 19xx

Last year			This year
£			£
412,600	**Sales**		475,000
49,000	Opening stock (on 1 July last year)	52,000
314,500	Add purchases	378,600
363,500		430,600
52,000	Less closing stock (on 30 June this year)	65,000
311,500	**Cost of goods sold**		365,600
101,100	**Gross profit** 23% (24.5% last year)		109,400
22,700	Staff wages		25,000
18,000	Rent		18,000
8,600	Rates		9,500
4,600	Heat and light		5,000
800	Telephone		900
900	Insurance		1,000
1,300	Professional fees		1,500
3,500	Motor expenses		4,000
3,800	Advertising		4,200
2,500	Repairs		3,000
1,400	Stationery and postage		1,500
3,000	Sundry expenses		2,800
71,100	**Total expenses**		76,400
2,000	**Interest:** loan	2,000
4,000	bank overdraft	5,000
		7,000
Depreciation: equipment, fixtures and fittings	6,000
9,000	motor vehicle	4,000	10,000
—	Loss on disposal of fixed asset		200
£15,000	**Net profit before tax**		£15,800
The net profit can be re-stated as	
13,100	Proprietor's salary		14,400
1,900	'Super profit'		1,400
£15,000			£15,800

despatched or services performed during the period, *not* just the cash you have received.

Cost of goods sold £365,600

From your sales, you must deduct the cost of providing or producing what you sell. This is called cost of goods sold and is the next figure down in the right-hand column.

Most accountants use the term 'cost of sales' rather than 'cost of goods sold'. Both terms mean the same but laymen usually understand the latter term more easily.

If you sell goods, your cost of sales is the cost to you of the items you sell. If you provide services, your cost of sales is any material you use. If you employ staff whose time you sell, such as in a repair workshop, your cost of sales may be mostly wages.

Cost of sales or cost of goods sold therefore means those of your costs which vary directly in proportion to your sales. In most businesses the only cost which varies directly with sales is goods purchased or produced.

You arrive at the value sold or used up in sales during the year by adding to the stock you held at the start the goods you purchased, and then deducting the stocks you have left. This calculation is inset in the left-hand column between 'sales' and 'cost of goods sold'. The figures are explained below.

Stocks – opening £52,000, closing £65,000

The stock figure is the value of the goods held for sale to customers or of materials held for use in performing your services.

Stocks are valued at cost net of VAT (valued added tax) *not* at selling price. If you valued them at selling price you would be taking profit on them before you had sold them. Any items which are old, obsolete, in poor condition or held in excessive quantities in relation to sales should be priced down to realistic values.

Purchases £378,600

This is the value of goods net of VAT received between the two stock-taking dates, *not* the total of cash paid to creditors. This is because, when you count stock, you list what you have. Thus it is the invoice for goods you have had in which must be shown as purchases. It is net of any returns to suppliers. Discounts received from suppliers may be shown separately if important.

Gross profit £109,400

This is a key figure. It is the profit per item sold or service rendered after charging your cost of sales but before paying all your fixed costs such as rent, rates, electricity etc. Since your cost of goods sold should be roughly constant as a percentage of sales, so should your gross profit.

Gross profit is very important. If you do not have the right profit at the gross level, you cannot have it at the net. Suppose gross profit is 25 per cent of sales and net profit 10 per cent, a 1 per cent variation from 25 to 24 per cent looks trivial – it's only 4 per cent of your gross profit; but the same 1 per cent becomes 10 per cent of your net profit (1 per cent on 10 per cent).

In practice gross profit is never a constant percentage of sales, for various reasons. For example, as your sales rise you should obtain better buying terms; on the other hand, stock losses can make a large hole in your profit.

Some causes of stock losses are:

- damaged goods destroyed or sold off at lower prices
- natural losses by evaporation etc
- inaccurate measuring of quantities sold or pricing errors
- errors by you in invoicing where goods are sold on credit or by supplier when bought on credit
- fraud by customers (shoplifting etc)
- fraud by suppliers (wrong deliveries or inaccurate invoicing)
- fraud by staff (cash or goods taken; goods supplied to friends at wrong prices etc)

See Chapter 9 for more about gross profit.

Expenses (wages and other overheads as listed in the example) £76,400

These are the expenses of operating the business for the period. In some cases, such as wages, the cost is usually the same as cash paid out. But for bills, such as the telephone, which are incurred on credit, the cost for the period is the bills which relate to that period, *not* just those which happen to have been paid during it.

Similarly, some expenses are paid in advance. Rent, rates and insurance are examples, and for these, the cost is the proportion relating to the period of the accounts, not the total paid out.

Depreciation £10,000

Depreciation is a different sort of cost from the other expenses: there is no invoice in the books for it but it is a cost none the less. Many assets used in the business wear out over a period. Plant, equipment, fixtures, fittings and vehicles are examples. These are not written off when they are bought. Their cost is shown in the balance sheet, as explained in the next chapter under fixed assets. The objective of depreciation is to charge against profits the cost of the asset over its working life. When it is either sold or scrapped, the depreciation charged up to that date therefore represents profit set aside to replace it.

Note that the profit set aside may not be represented by cash. The cash may already have been used to finance other fixed assets, stocks, debtors etc. The reasons why profit is not necessarily the same as cash will become clearer as you read subsequent chapters.

Note also that since estimates or averages have to be used for each kind of asset, the amount is only an intelligent guess, not a precise forecast.

The depreciation is based upon historic cost. The price of a replacement item may have risen substantially owing to inflation, technological advances etc. So you might need to make extra provision for the replacement of assets over and above normal depreciation.

See the comments about fixed assets in the next two chapters for more about different methods of calculating depreciation.

The loss on disposal of fixed assets, £200, is the book value of an item which was scrapped. That means the value to which it had been written down by depreciation. As it was scrapped, not sold, the entire book value was a loss. Had, say, £120 been obtained for it, the loss would have been £80.

Net profit before tax £15,800

I re-state this as you can see in the example. Proprietor's (or director's) salary represents the wage of the owner manager.

When looking at how you are doing, make a realistic estimate of what you could earn in a job. Only if there is a surplus are you earning a 'super profit' which is the real return you obtain from your investment in the business. It is the correct figure to compare with the return you could obtain by selling the business, investing the proceeds and taking a job. Express your 'super profit' as a percentage of your interest in the business and you have the real reward for all the extra sweat of being the boss.

See Chapters 9 and 10 for more comments on how the fall in gross profit has hit the real return earned by the owner of this business, reducing it to a miserable figure.

Questions

Check your answers with the text.

- Does the sales figure include VAT?
- Does the stock valuation include VAT?
- Is the purchases figure:
  (a) value of goods received in the period, or
  (b) value of invoices received in the period, or
  (c) total of cash paid to suppliers in the period?
- What does the cost of goods sold figure represent?
- What are the causes of stock losses? (Give at least five.)
- What is gross profit?

Chapter 5

The Balance Sheet Explained

Now we come to the second statement which makes up a set of accounts – the balance sheet.

Read this chapter in conjunction with the example for the XYZ shop on page 35. If you own or work for a limited company, you will also need to read Chapter 6 on the accounts of a limited company, since there are differences between the accounts for sole traders or partnerships and those of limited companies. Read this one first, however, because various points are common to all businesses.

As already explained in Chapter 3, the balance sheet shows where the business has got to at the date on which the profit and loss account ends. It is, if you like, a snapshot of the business at that moment. In contrast, the profit and loss account can be likened to a video of the events during the year. The balance sheet begins with what the business owns, its assets, and deducts its liabilities, to arrive at the net value, the proprietor's interest. This order is not always the same. Some accountants put the proprietor's interest (for a limited company the share capital) at the top.

There are three kinds of assets: fixed, intangible and current.

Fixed assets £49,800

These are the items which the business buys to retain for use over a long period, rather than resell at a profit. They are usually kept until they wear out, become obsolete or are no longer suitable for the business. Examples are buildings, plant, equipment, fixtures and fittings, and vehicles. The layout shown here for fixed assets is that usually adopted for sole traders or partnerships. For limited companies, see Chapter 6. For convenience, the details are shown in the balance sheet in the example, but they are usually in a separate note. The net book value (NBV) is the balance remaining after deducting, from the NBV at the start of the year, the depreciation as shown in the profit and loss

THE XYZ SHOP
Balance sheet at 30 June 19XX
(vertical layout)

Last year		Net book value start of year	Bought in year	Sales in year	Deprecia-tion for year	This year Net book value end of year
£	**Fixed assets**	£	£	£	£	£
22,000	Equipment	22,000	6,000	200	5,000	22,800
20,000	Fixtures	20,000	—	—	2,000	18,000
12,000	Vehicle	12,000	—	—	3,000	9,000
54,000		54,000	6,000	200	10,000	49,800
6,000	**Goodwill**					6,000
	Current assets					
52,300	Stock (trade £65,000: other £300)				65,300	
9,700	Accounts receivable (debtors)				10,700	
1,800	Payments in advance				2,000	
63,800						78,000
123,800	**Total assets**					133,800
	Less:					
	Current liabilities due within one year					
13,500	Accounts payable (creditors)				16,000	
2,500	Future tax payable				3,000	
30,000	Bank overdraft				34,200	
46,000						53,200
	Creditors due after one year					
20,000	Loan					20,000
£57,800	**Proprietor's interest in the business**					60,600
	Represented by:					
54,800	Balance of capital at start of year					57,800
12,500	Add profit for year (after tax of £3,000)					12,800
67,300						70,600
9,500	Deduct drawings					10,000
£57,800	**Balance of capital at end of year**					£60,600

account. Additions and sales of assets during the year are also shown. The depreciation is calculated for a full year on the starting NBV, after deducting any sales and proportionately on items bought during the year. This is called the 'reducing balance' method of depreciating and, since a percentage of the reducing total is written off, the assets are never fully depreciated. It is simple to use, and it is not necessary to keep records of each item in order to show when it is written off. An alternative, the 'straight line' method, is explained in Chapter 6.

Intangible assets

These include goodwill, patent, trade-mark or royalty rights and other items for which cash is paid but which have no tangible form.

Goodwill £6,000

In the example, the proprietor of the business paid £6,000 for goodwill when he bought it. That is to say, the price he paid exceeded by £6,000 the value of the net assets he took over. Net assets are fixtures and fittings, equipment, stock, debtors etc, less any liabilities to creditors etc, for which he accepted responsibility.

People are often confused about goodwill. It is not an identifiable asset with its own value. It is in effect a balancing figure arrived at as follows.

Say you are offered a business earning a net profit of £20,000. You are prepared to pay 1½ years' profits for it, plus stock at valuation. You are therefore buying the leasehold, fixed assets and goodwill for £30,000. If the fixed assets are valued at £26,000 you are paying £4,000 for the right to the leasehold (not usually separated from goodwill) and the goodwill. If any debtors or creditors were taken over they would, of course, be a part of the calculation.

However, the value of the fixed assets always depends upon the view you take of them. If you value them for use as they stand in a going concern, they are worth far more than if you tried to sell them off as surplus. So the balancing figure taken as the value of goodwill is arbitrary. One cannot value goodwill for itself – only as a consequence of deciding what one will pay for a given amount of profit and then deducting one's valuation of fixed assets and current assets, if applicable, from the price paid.

Current assets £78,000

These are the items arising and constantly changing in the course of trading. Examples are stocks which convert into debtors which become cash. Note that 'other' stocks are such items as stationery or fuel. 'Trade' stocks are goods for resale or for use in manufacturing other goods.

Liabilities

Liabilities are long term or short term. Long-term liabilities are amounts repayable more than a year ahead such as loans, mortgages etc; but *not* a bank overdraft because this is repayable on demand.

Current liabilities £53,200

These are amounts repayable within one year such as creditors, bank overdrafts, short-term loans etc.

Accounts receivable or payable (debtors and creditors)

A debtor owes you money. You owe money to a creditor. It may help you to distinguish between them if you recall that it is the creditors of a business who force it into liquidation. One talks of a creditors' winding up, not a debtors' one.

More about stocks

For a retailer or wholesaler, stocks consist of the goods he deals in. A manufacturer often has various kinds of stock such as:

- raw materials
- bought-in parts and sub-assemblies
- work in progress
- finished goods
- stationery, advertising and sales promotion materials, fuel etc.

These are explained below.

Raw materials

One man's finished goods are another man's raw materials. Raw materials are those goods which a business buys in order to transform them by its production processes into finished products. Examples are the timber, nails, glue etc bought by a furniture manufacturer or the powders, perfumes and chemicals used by a cosmetics manufacturer.

Bought-in parts

Many businesses buy in parts for use in assembling their products. For instance, the cosmetics manufacturer buys in jars and pots in which to put his lotions and creams and the car manufacturer purchases sparking plugs for his engines. Such parts are often distinguished from raw materials by being called bought-in parts, components or even sub-assemblies.

Sub-assemblies are sections of a product put together by a supplier specifically for the manufacturer. A car manufacturer, for instance, might buy in complete door handle and window winding assemblies for his car doors.

Sub-assemblies may also be sections of a product put together by the manufacturer himself and awaiting the next stage in the production process. In this case they will very likely be classified as work in progress.

Work in progress

Work in progress stocks are those which are part-way through the production cycle. For example, a motor vehicle is assembled through various stages. Since the production process is continuous, there are bound to be unfinished vehicles at the date of taking stock.

The term 'work in progress' is also used to describe work done on unfinished construction contracts. In a service industry or a professional office such as that of an accountant or an architect, work in progress is the time spent on jobs which have not yet been charged to the customer or the client because the work is incomplete.

Finished goods (or, in the USA, 'inventory')

Finished goods are stocks ready for sale to customers. This does not necessarily mean that they are goods which the ultimate customer would recognise. The sub-assembly bought by a car manufacturer for his car door is 'finished goods' to the business which makes it, even though it is several stages away from the state in which the car reaches the showroom.

Stationery, advertising and sales promotion materials, heating fuel etc
These goods are overhead expenses of most businesses rather than part of the direct cost of goods bought or produced for resale. Expenditure on them is shown in the profit and loss account as an expense, not as part of cost of sales.

Sales promotional materials are items such as sales brochures, catalogues, sales stands for shop counters and so on.

Once incurred, an expense normally has no residual value, unlike a production cost which produces stock. Often, therefore, stocks of stationery, advertising and sales promotion materials, fuel etc, are ignored. If the value of such stocks is significant, however, they can be counted and included in the balance sheet. This is often done if a large bill has been incurred just before the end of the financial year for goods which will mostly be used during the following year.

The charge to the expense heading in the profit and loss account is then the total of bills received for the goods in question less the value of the stocks carried forward to the next accounting period (plus any stocks brought forward from the previous accounting period).

Proprietor's interest in the business £60,600

This represents the cash originally put in plus profits, less taxation and drawings and any losses. In the balance sheet of a limited company it is shown as share capital and reserves, the total of which belongs to the shareholders. Individual directors, who may or may not be the shareholders, may have amounts owing to them on current account as well but these sums are current liabilities. 'Drawings' of a profit for a company are dividends to the shareholders. If the directors own the company, they may of course draw profit as salaries rather than as dividends.

In a partnership, and sometimes for a sole trader, a distinction is made between permanent capital and current account balances of profits not drawn. The total of capital and current balances is then the proprietor's interest.

Expressed slightly differently, the owner's interest is the value of what the business owns less what it owes to outsiders.

THE BALANCE SHEET EXPLAINED

THE XYZ SHOP
Balance sheet at 30 June 19XX
(horizontal layout)

Capital

Last year £		This year £
54,800	Balance of capital at start of year	57,800
12,500	Add profit for year (after tax of £3,000)	12,800
67,300		70,600
9,500	Deduct drawings	10,000
57,800	Proprietor's interest in the business	60,600

Creditors due after one year

Last year £		This year £
20,000	Loan	20,000

Current liabilities due within one year

Last year			This year	
13,500	Accounts payable (creditors)	16,000		
2,500	Future tax payable	3,000		
30,000	Bank overdraft	34,200		
46,000			53,200	
£123,800			£133,800	

Fixed assets

Last year £	Fixed assets	Net book value start of year £	Bought in year £	Sales in year £	Depreciation for year £	This year Net book value end of year £
22,000	Equipment	22,000	6,000	200	5,000	22,800
20,000	Fixtures	20,000	—	—	2,000	18,000
12,000	Vehicle	12,000	—	—	3,000	9,000
54,000		54,000	6,000	200	10,000	49,800
6,000	Goodwill					6,000

Current assets

Last year			This year
52,000	Stock (trade £64,700: other £300)		65,000
10,000	Accounts receivable (debtors)		11,000
1,800	Payments in advance		2,000
63,800			78,000
£123,800			£133,800

'Vertical' or 'horizontal' layout

The proprietor's interest is a liability of the business to him. This is why, in a 'horizontal' layout of a balance sheet, it appears in the liabilities. The same figures used for the sample 'vertical' balance sheet are re-laid out as in the 'horizontal' layout shown because some accountants use this form.

Questions

Check your answers with the text.

- What are:
  - (a) fixed assets
  - (b) intangible assets and goodwill
  - (c) current assets
  - (d) long-term liabilities
  - (e) current liabilities
  - (f) proprietor's interest in the business?
- What kinds of stock are there? (Five are discussed.)

Chapter 6

The Accounts of a Limited Company

This chapter discusses how the accounts of a small limited company differ from those of a sole trader or a partnership. In Chapter 2 I explained the legal distinctions which the accounts reflect. We'll discuss the accounts of big companies later in the book. At present we are looking at the figures for a small business which happens to be a limited company, ABC Ltd. You will need to have read Chapters 4 and 5 because many of the headings are the same and I comment only on the differences.

The profit and loss account

This book explains the figures in your accounts which you can use in running your business; it is not primarily concerned with the formalities of presentation which the law requires. When you start to read an actual set of accounts, you will find they are more complicated than my examples, because all limited companies, big or small, are subject to rules in the Companies Acts as to the information which they must show in their accounts.

The example of a profit and loss account in Chapter 4 shows the detailed information which is included in the management accounts for a small business if it produces its own figures. If the accounts are done by professional accountants, as they often are for small companies owned by their directors, a detailed profit and loss account is included in the copies for the owners. The accounts sent to the Registrar of Companies will omit it, however.

In the published accounts for the Registrar and outside shareholders, if there are any, the profit and loss account has only to give certain figures, such as sales, cost of sales, totals for certain headings, such as selling and administration expenses and various specific costs, including salaries and wages, interest and the audit fee. In practice, much of this information is given in notes rather than in the profit and loss account or the balance sheet itself.

Very small companies can choose a simplified presentation for the figures, which they send to the Registrar of Companies, giving even fewer details.

You need to know all this only so that you are not confused when you try to compare these examples with a real set of accounts, which will seem much more complex. It isn't really, once you understand the idea, and you should find you can follow the presentation required by law when you have got the feel of mine.

Some differences in the figures for a company
The profit and loss account for a company differs from the example for a sole trader, which we have already looked at, in two important ways. First, the directors, being employees of the company, are paid salaries. This expense is shown either with or adjacent to the staff costs for other employees.

Thus the figure of profit shown below is after paying the directors whereas, for a sole trader, the profit is before his drawings – all the profit belongs to him. In the case of a company, the profit belongs to the shareholders, who may not be the same people as the directors. Hence the need to charge the latter's pay before arriving at the profit before tax. Second, there may be a dividend paid to the shareholders.

Last year			This year
£			£
80,000	Net profit before tax		100,000
20,000	Less corporation tax		30,000
60,000	Net profit after tax		70,000
5,000	Less preference dividend		5,000
	Ordinary dividend interim already paid	£10,000	
24,000	final proposed	£20,000	30,000
31,000	Balance of profit undistributed for year		35,000
	Add balance brought forward from previous		
18,000	years		49,000
	Balance of profit undistributed carried		
£49,000	forward (see balance sheet on page 46)		£84,000

This example assumes that there are outside shareholders in the company who require dividends on their shares. If the shareholders are all directors, they may prefer to draw the profits as directors' salaries, rather than dividends, for tax reasons.

Shares are explained later and dividends in the next chapter.

In this example, the company has a profit of £70,000 available after tax for distribution to shareholders or for retention in the company. Dividends either paid or proposed take £35,000, leaving £35,000 retained to add to the accumulated balance of previous retentions.

Is the profit retention of £35,000 cash in the bank?

Retained profits are not necessarily cash in the bank. The money may well have been used already to finance increased stocks or receivables (debtors), as is the case in this example. The company has an overdraft, as we shall see from the balance sheet a little further on. The reason for this is explained in later chapters.

How much profit should be retained?

Profit is not available to be taken out of a business until it results in cash in the bank. Even then you must leave money in your business to finance it, especially if your sales are growing and you must build up resources for a rainy day.

The need to retain the profit varies from company to company and, to some extent, from trade to trade. Some industries, particularly manufacturers, have to invest more heavily in new equipment and require more working capital to finance stock or debtors in order to stay in business than others. More sales mean more stock and more credit to customers which absorbs cash. This is further explained in later chapters.

Industries such as the furniture, building and construction industries tend to be cyclical, with good and bad years succeeding each other, as the economy changes. Such companies cannot pay out a high proportion of profits as dividends in good years if they are to maintain the dividend in poor ones. They tend, therefore, to retain a high proportion of profit in the good years to provide a cushion for the bad times when they may have difficulty in earning enough to 'cover' the dividend.

A few industries, such as retailing, tend to pay out a higher proportion of profit because they are more static. The business is more stable and swings in profits are less violent. If the company is well run, much of a retailer's working capital is provided by credit from his suppliers. A good proportion of his stocks can be sold for cash before or around the date on which he has to pay for them. He can therefore afford to pay out a higher proportion of profits and indeed often needs to do so because the attraction of his shares to an investor is more likely to be a secure steady income than the prospect of rapidly increasing profits.

Of course, the best companies in an industry tend to be exceptions to such general statements. Equally the financial situation of the company often dictates the policy. It may be necessary to plough back more profit than usual for several years to finance expansion. On the other hand, a high dividend may have to be paid in order to persuade the shareholders to invest fresh capital to pay for expansion because there is no way that the company can generate enough cash from its existing business.

The balance sheet

The example on the next page is similar to that of a sole trader or partnership but there are various differences of detail.

What is share capital?

It will help you to understand these notes if we deal first with share capital. It is not the first figure in the example but, since you must know what it is in order to follow the points made about other entries, it is dealt with first. So we start with the shareholders' interest.

Share capital – ordinary shares £45,000

As explained in Chapter 2 a company issues 'shares' as a receipt for the money put in by its shareholders. These shares can be sold by one shareholder to another or to a third party either privately, or, if the shares are 'quoted', through the Stock Exchange.

Sometimes shares are issued in return for assets transferred to the company rather than for cash paid into its bank account.

If the company is a private one, the transfer of its shares is often subject to control by the directors who have power to refuse to register the transfer to a person of whom they do not approve.

Instead of shares, the word 'stock' is sometimes used. Ordinary stock means the same thing as ordinary shares; do not confuse this with loan stock, which means a loan on fixed interest terms.

ABC Limited
Balance sheet at 30 June 19XX

Last year		Original cost	Accumu-lated depreciation	This year Net book value
£	**Fixed assets**	£	£	£
87,400	Equipment	104,000	21,000	83,000
30,000	Fixtures and fittings	33,000	6,000	27,000
30,000	Vehicles	49,000	24,000	25,000
147,400		186,000	51,000	135,000
—	**Patents and trade marks**			30,000
15,000	**Goodwill**			15,000
57,000	**Investment in associated company**			57,000
	Current assets			
180,000	Stocks (trade £195,000: other £5,000		200,000	
29,000	Accounts receivable (debtors)		33,000	
8,600	Payments in advance		9,000	
217,600				242,000
437,000	**Total assets**			479,000
	Less:			
	Current liabilities due within one year			
80,000	Accounts payable (creditors)		82,000	
23,000	Current tax payable		32,000	
14,000	Ordinary dividend due (final only)		20,000	
110,000	Bank overdraft		93,000	
227,000			227,000	
15,000	**Deferred taxation**			13,000
	Creditors due after one year			
30,000	Loan			30,000
£165,000	**Shareholders' interest in the business**			£209,000
	Represented by:			
	Share capital and reserves			
45,000	Ordinary shares of £1 (authorised £60,000)			45,000
50,000	10% preference shares of £1			50,000
30,000	Capital reserve			30,000
40,000	Balance of undistributed profit			84,000
£165,000				£209,000

The ordinary shares usually control the company with one vote per share but there are sometimes different classes of ordinary share with different voting rights. Often these special shares are called 'A' shares. They may have no votes at all or they could have, say, ten times as many as the rest of the shares. The voting rights are fixed as part of the terms on which they are offered to shareholders and the reason for different rights is usually to preserve the status quo of control of the company.

The significance of voting rights is that he who controls over 50 per cent of the votes controls the company and can appoint the directors. For complete control, over 90 per cent of the votes is needed. The Companies Acts lay down different percentages which are needed to do different things such as change voting rights, repay share capital etc, but 51 per cent gives control of the day-to-day management of the business.

What is authorised capital?

Shares can be issued at any time in return for money, or for an asset acquired by the company, up to the limit of its authorised capital. Once the authorised limit has been reached, the shareholders must approve any increase in it. Such an increase then remains available for issue as required. Thus, in the example, the company has an authorised capital of £60,000 but has only issued £45,000 of it.

Share capital is not cash

This is not to say that the company has £15,000 spare cash. When they authorise a given figure of share capital, the shareholders merely fix a limit upon the powers of the directors. No value is received by the company until it actually issues the shares.

Preference shares £50,000

A company sometimes has preference shares as well as ordinary shares. Preference shares are entitled only to a fixed percentage dividend – 10 per cent in the example (based on their nominal value – not on the value quoted on the Stock Exchange or elsewhere). The dividend is only payable if the directors consider that the profits (and cash position) are adequate but it ranks in priority before any dividend on the ordinary shares. Normally preference shares have no votes but often they obtain them if their dividend is not paid and this can result in the control of the company changing hands, depending upon the respective voting rights of the ordinary and preference shares.

Some preference dividends are cumulative until all arrears are cleared. Others are non-cumulative and the dividends are lost if not paid for any year.

If the company is wound up, the preference shares rank before the ordinary shares for repayment up to their nominal value. They can, however, be repaid without winding up the company if a majority of the holders agree; the ordinary shares, on the other hand, can only be repaid if the company is either wound up or reconstructed, which is a complicated legal process.

What does 'nominal value' of loan stock and ordinary shares mean?

The nominal value of loan stock or of shares is the figure which appears in the balance sheet of the issuing company and represents the amount it owes to the holders. In the case of loan stock or preference shares, this is the amount repayable as and when the stock is redeemed or the shares are repaid.

In the case of ordinary shares, however, nominal value is merely the original value fixed for the shares. Since the ordinary shareholders are entitled to the profits remaining after paying all fixed interest and preference dividends, it follows that, should the company be sold or wound up, the ordinary shareholders receive the net proceeds remaining after meeting all other obligations. This may be greater or less than the nominal value of their shares, depending on whether the company has made a profit or loss since the shares were issued. If the company is forced into liquidation by its creditors, the shareholders often receive nothing.

What is the actual value of shares?

The nominal value of shares, both ordinary and preference and of loan stock, has little bearing on their value if sold by one investor to another. The price obtainable, whether on the Stock Exchange or elsewhere, depends upon investors' expectations as to the income obtainable, the security of it, the possibility, for ordinary shares, of its increasing in the future and their assessment of the investment in comparison with the rates of return available elsewhere.

If a shareholding is large enough to justify a directorship for the holder, this increases its value, particularly in the case of a private company. The holder of 51 per cent of the shares of the private company can often largely ignore the wishes of the minority holders and, in consequence, the latter's shares may be very difficult to sell at anything near the value per share of the majority holding.

Reserves – capital £30,000; profit and loss £84,000

A capital reserve is a profit on a capital asset, such as property. It is not always realised. An unrealised profit results from re-valuing assets up from cost to the estimated present value. An actual sale produces a realised profit.

A capital reserve is not usually distributed by way of dividend. Indeed there are legal restrictions on doing so. For one thing the profit must be a realised one. Anyway, the money is often needed to finance the business.

A revenue reserve is available for distribution. It represents the balance of profits earned in previous years but not distributed. Often it is really the additional funds needed to let the company grow, and is permanent capital just as much as the share capital or capital reserves. If that is so, the cash is not available to pay out because it is tied up in stocks or other assets.

The difference between a reserve and a provision

A reserve is part of the shareholders' funds and represents profit tucked away to help finance the company and in case of a rainy day. A provision is an amount set aside to meet a specific liability. One example is the provision for deferred taxation explained later; another is a provision for bad debts which is an amount deducted from the profits in anticipation that some customers will not pay up.

Having explained the items which make up the shareholders' interest, we now go back to the example on page 46.

Fixed assets £186,000 − £51,000 = £135,000

Company law requires the original cost of the assets to be shown. This is therefore the first column in the example. The second column shows the accumulated depreciation written off to date for the years in which the assets have been owned. The third column shows the net book value of £135,000.

These totals cannot, of course, show any additions or sales during the year and the total of any such changes have to be given in a separate note to the accounts. The accumulated depreciation figure includes the charge for the year shown in the profit and loss account.

Depreciation for a limited company is usually charged on the 'straight line' basis. Thus, a charge of 25 per cent on the original cost will write off an item over four years. This is in contrast to, say 33⅓ per cent on the reducing balance, which, although a higher percentage, never completely writes it off, as explained in the comment on fixed assets in Chapter 5.

Office equipment, machinery etc is usually depreciated over ten years, except for computers which become obsolete so quickly that as little as three years may be appropriate. Cars are normally written off over four years; even though they are expected to fetch a substantial proportion of their original price when sold, second-hand prices fluctuate considerably and, as the replacement is sure to cost more than the old vehicle did, it is wise to write off too much rather than too little.

The cost of any leases of buildings has to be written off over the remaining period of the lease. This also applies to expenditure on fixtures and fittings which will not be removable if you have to vacate the premises. Freehold buildings are also supposed to be depreciated now following a recommendation by the professional accounting bodies. However, this is contentious and only public companies are likely to do so, usually at 2 per cent per annum.

If an item has been sold, the difference between the net book value and the price obtained will be shown in the profit and loss account as a profit (or loss) on sale of fixed assets. If the item has been scrapped, the whole of the net book value is a loss unless, of course, it was already fully depreciated and therefore in the books at a net value of nil. The most frequent such figure to appear is the profit or loss on the sale of a motor vehicle.

To use the straight line method accurately, the records of the company must show the total additions separately for each year so that after, say, ten years at 10 per cent, the additions for 1981 are no longer depreciated in 1991. Provided that one knows when an item was bought, it is easy to calculate how much depreciation has been charged by the year in which it is sold, or scrapped. Even if the original cost is not known, it can be estimated and the totals for original cost and accumulated depreciation adjusted to reflect the sale. Without such figures year by year, one cannot tell how much of the assets is fully written off.

Plant registers help to keep track of fixed assets

Vehicles are easy to keep track of but individual machines and equipment can become merged as part of general plant, particularly if moved about. Many companies therefore number plant and keep a plant register so as to identify individual items as to age, specification, cost etc.

Without such a register, it can be difficult to identify the original cost of an item, which has to be taken out of the fixed assets total when it is sold. After a few years, it becomes impossible to reconcile the total in the balance sheet with the individual assets owned. Plant registers are therefore important in the larger company as an aid to keeping tabs on what the business owns.

Patents and trade marks £30,000

The company has acquired some patents and trade marks during the last year. The £30,000 cost could either be the purchase price or the expenses incurred if the company has designed and registered its own patent or mark.

Investment in associated company £57,000

An associated company is one in which the investing company effectively has a say in the management policy and has a director on the other company's board either because it is a partner or because it owns at least 20 per cent of the shares.

Since the investing company can influence the dividends paid to it, the investment is distinguished as 'associated' rather than 'trade'. Both 'associated' and 'trade' investments are held for the longer term but shares can also be held as a short-term home for spare funds, in which case they are treated as a current asset rather than separated, as here.

The investment in an associated company might include the cost of buying shares in it or long-term loans made to it. Any sums due from it for ordinary sales to it, or payable to it for ordinary purchases from it, on normal trade terms, are shown as 'amounts due from (or to) associated companies' in current assets or current liabilities. Under company law, such sums 'in the family' must not be hidden away in ordinary debtors or creditors.

Investments in subsidiary companies

A subsidiary company is one in which your company owns more than half the shares. It therefore controls it for practical purposes. There is no such investment in the example. Companies invest in other companies for many reasons, such as to diversify activities by starting new ones or buying existing operations, to defend themselves against their competitors or to form an alliance with suppliers or customers.

Goodwill was explained in Chapter 5.

Current tax payable £32,000

This is the tax due shortly as opposed to the provision for deferred taxation (see below).

Ordinary dividend due £20,000

This is the final dividend. The interim dividend was paid during the year as a payment on account. The directors can pay an interim dividend if they are satisfied that profits will cover it, but the final one needs approval by the shareholders at the annual general meeting.

Deferred taxation £13,000

Deferred taxation means tax which will be payable in the future. It is provided for as a liability at the time the profit is earned to show the profit after tax undistorted by tax fluctuations. These arise when the depreciation charged in the profit and loss account is not the same as the amount permitted for corporation tax.

Does your company have departmental accounts?

A substantial company may well have a number of different departments or activities. It will want to know how its sales, expenses and profits compare for these and its accounts may therefore be in several sections. However many different operating statements there may be in your company, you will see that they build up to a similar overall statement as shown in the earlier example even though much of the detail is on departmental schedules.

Questions

Check your answers with the text.

- What items does one find in a profit and loss appropriation account?
- What governs how much profit a business needs to retain?
- What is the meaning of the following:
  share capital
  authorised capital
  preference shares
  investments in associated companies?
- What is the difference between current and deferred tax?

Chapter 7

How the Figures in the Profit and Loss Account are Arrived at

The sum for each item in the profit and loss account is the amount of income earned or expense incurred during the period. This is a simple idea to grasp in theory, but do you understand what it means in practice? Here are three examples. The answers follow.

Sales

If all your sales are for cash – that is to say, if your customers hand over money (or a cheque) when you give them the goods or service – the total of your sales is the cash received.

But if you allow credit to your customers, is the sales figure:

(a) the total value of the goods and services which you deliver to them in the period (the value of any deliveries not yet invoiced being estimated)?

(b) the total of the invoices which you issue to them in the period?

(c) the total cash you receive from customers in the period?

Purchase of goods for resale

If your suppliers allow you credit, is the value of your purchases:

(a) the value of goods received from suppliers in the period (the value of any deliveries not yet invoiced being estimated)?

(b) the value of the invoices received from suppliers in the period?

(c) the total of cash paid to suppliers in the period?

Expenses

An 'expense' is an item of cost incurred in running a business, such as rent, rates, telephone etc, as opposed to goods bought for resale to customers.

For example, is the cost of the telephone:

(a) the value of the bills received in the period?
(b) the value of bills received as adjusted by an estimate for any period not covered by invoices to hand?
(c) the total cash paid to the telephone service?

For both sales and purchases (a) and (b) may be the same figures but this depends on whether your own and your suppliers' invoicing is up to date. The longer you wait before closing your records for the period, the fewer any missing invoices will be.

Try to work out the answers before you read on.

Answers
The answers are: Sales (a); Purchase of goods (a) and Expenses (b). Here's why.

It is a common mistake to think of money as being earned or spent when the payment is made: in fact, this is often just the settlement of a sale which was achieved or a debt which was incurred much earlier.

The bank account shows the money coming in and the money going out, but this is no guide to the profit. To show the true position, we must allow for sales and liabilities for which we have not yet received the cash or for which we have not yet paid.

When is a sale a sale?

If you sell services, it is the date the work is completed which determines the accounting period into which the sale goes. All services provided up to the end of each period must either be invoiced or their value to date estimated as 'work in progress'. If you sell goods, the sale is made when they are delivered to the customer.

Sometimes a contract provides for progress payments prior to delivery. Credit for the sale is usually then taken in stages rather than on delivery though this depends upon the nature of the contract.

Watch your 'cut off' of goods against invoice

If you sell goods on credit, you must match the despatch of the goods with the invoices you issue. You would be taking a double profit if the goods were to be counted in stock and invoices for them also included in the sales. All goods which are despatched by the end of the accounting period must therefore be invoiced and included in your total accounts receivable (debtors); conversely, goods still held are counted as stock and the invoice is dated in the following period in which they are

This procedure is sometimes called the 'cut off' because it determines the point at which you stop invoicing for one period and start for the next. The same procedure works in reverse for purchases of goods for resale.

When is a purchase a purchase?

Goods received before stock-taking will be included in the value of stocks counted: therefore the corresponding liability to the supplier must be included in accounts payable (creditors).

On the other hand, we do not want to include any suppliers' invoices in accounts payable unless the goods have been counted in stock.

This can only be done accurately if the suppliers' delivery notes are marked with the dates of receipt of the goods. Subsequently, these documents are matched with the invoices received from suppliers. It is sometimes necessary to estimate the value of invoices outstanding at the end of the accounting period in cases where suppliers are very slow to invoice.

Conversely, the date of receipt of any goods received after stock-taking should be marked on the delivery notes to prevent the invoices being included in accounts payable. The invoice belongs to the following accounting period because the goods have not been counted in stock.

This procedure for ensuring that invoices for goods bought are charged to the correct accounting period is especially important because the sums of money involved are often large in relation to other figures in the accounts. If the 'cut off' is wrong the profit margin percentage may well be seriously distorted. If this is not realised, the accounts may be misleading and cause wrong decisions to be taken.

Example
Suppose the stock includes goods received just before stock-

taking to the value of £1,000, for which no corresponding invoice is included in accounts payable. As a result, the cost of goods sold is reduced and the profit is increased.

If sales are £50,000, an extra £1,000 profit is 2 per cent. If this makes the gross profit margin appear in the accounts as 20 per cent when the real figure is 18 per cent an owner who expected, say, 21 per cent, could then be misled. He might well accept a 1 per cent drop when he ought to be investigating one of 3 per cent.

Remember that 'purchases' and 'cost of goods sold' are not the same

As explained in Chapter 4 the purchase total is adjusted by opening and closing stocks so as to charge against sales the cost of goods *sold*.

Expenses

In the case of services bought in, such as electricity, telephone etc, it is often necessary to estimate the amount due for the period from the date to which the last invoice received was made up to the end of the accounting period.

Deposits received in advance

Some businesses take deposits or payments in advance from customers. Where money has been received in advance of the services being performed or the goods supplied, the amounts outstanding must be listed and carried forward as payments in advance from customers. Otherwise the profits will be inflated and too much tax may be payable, quite apart from the accounts failing to show a fair view of the position.

Thus the figures relating to the period covered by a profit and loss account are not necessarily just the cash you have paid or the invoices you have issued or received. Often these figures need adjusting to make them show the full story, not just those bits of it which happen to have been recorded so far.

The same principle applies for expenses. We must charge against profits the cost for the period, which is not necessarily what we have paid out.

How the arithmetic works for a small business which keeps records on a cash basis

If yours is a small business and you do not keep a full set of accounting records, this is how your accountant will work out your sales:

	£
Cash received during the period; say	100,000
Less accounts receivable at start of period	10,000
(ie debtors – amounts owing to you)	
	£90,000
Add accounts receivable at the end of the period	
(the reverse of the above)	8,000
Sales for period	£98,000

If the accounts receivable at the start have been paid during the period, they will be included in the total of cash receipts above. Since they relate to sales in the previous period, we deduct them. If there are any still unpaid, they will be added back as part of the total still receivable at the end of the period.

If there were any goods delivered or, if you sell services, there were jobs completed by the end of the period which had not been invoiced, the value should be added in the total of accounts receivable so as to be part of the sales.

The purchases calculation is the same but uses the totals of money paid out and accounts payable (creditors – amounts owing by you) at the start and end of the period thus producing the figure of purchases of goods for resale received in the period.

Summary

The objective of the profit and loss account is to show the profits earned during the period from the sales made to customers and to charge the correct expenses both for goods 'used up' in supplies to customers and for services consumed in running the business during the period, regardless of whether invoices have been raised or payments made. It is whether or not a liability has been incurred which decides whether a cost is a charge against the profit. The actual payment, in cash or by cheque, is merely the settlement of that liability.

Questions

- Return to the first page of this chapter and revise the questions there.

Chapter 8

Points on the Accounts of a Public Company

Here are a few more points which may help you understand the accounts of large companies. This is not a treatise on public company accounts, but just the aspects which are most important for the layman and beginner to know about.

What do the published accounts of a company show?

As explained in Chapter 6, the Companies Acts do not require a detailed profit and loss account to be issued to shareholders or to be filed at Companies House. Your company's annual report may well be an expensive glossy production, but you will find that it does not show very much detailed information about sales and expenses when compared with internal management accounts. The latter contain confidential details which do not have to be made public.

Why are dividends paid to shareholders?

The ordinary shareholders take the biggest risk. They are the first to suffer if things go wrong and, should the company go out of business, they are the last to be paid after all the other creditors and lenders to the company. In return for their risk, they are entitled to all the surplus, should profits be made. In practice they cannot take all this out of the company both for tax reasons and because the business needs retained profit. Just as you expect interest on your savings in a building society or bank deposit account, the shareholder needs an income from his much higher risk investment. He does not always get it. He only receives dividends provided that there is enough *cash* to spare, not just profit. He is taxed on these dividends as unearned private income.

If the directors are also the shareholders, they may prefer to take their share of profits as salaries rather than as dividends.

Sometimes a director, who is a major shareholder, waives his right to a dividend thus allowing other shareholders, who are not directors, to receive an income while leaving more cash in the company.

Is a dividend of £30,000 on share capital of £45,000 'big money'?

This is the figure from the example in Chapter 6 (pages 43 and 46). It is not what it seems. This comparison is with the nominal value of the shares which is the amount originally invested by the shareholders. This may have been many years ago in which case the profits retained in the company each year will have built up to substantial sums. These reserves are often as much as or even substantially greater than the nominal share capital.

The successful investment of these accumulated reserves will have increased the annual profit. The dividend will therefore have risen as well. If you re-calculate it as a percentage of the total shareholders' funds including reserves, you will find that it is much lower and that in many cases it represents no more than a modest return to the investor on his true investment. Here the shareholders' interest is £209,000 (see balance sheet).

In the case of a quoted company the Stock Exchange price for the shares may or may not be close to their value as shown by the balance sheet, depending upon the popularity or otherwise of the shares. The return to the investor is his dividend as a percentage of the price of his shares and it can be as low as 2 or 3 per cent even in a depressed share market. Only if there is serious doubt about the company's future profits will the dividend yield on the share price go much above 10 per cent. So high nominal dividends are not what they seem.

Dividend 'cover'

In some sets of accounts, the accumulated balance on the profit and loss account is added to the profit after tax before showing the dividends paid. This has the effect of hiding the key point of dividend 'cover', ie how much is paid out in dividends compared with the amount of profit retained.

In the example the cover is £65,000 (after the preference dividend) for £30,000 or about twice as much; see page 43.

Consolidated balance sheets

If a company has one or more subsidiaries (or 'associated' companies), they form a group of companies. None of the balance sheets of the individual companies will show the total value of the group. In the example previously explained, the holding company shows only the value of its investment in its subsidiaries or associates at cost. This may not reflect the real value, particularly if the investment was made some years ago.

For this reason a consolidated balance sheet is prepared for a group of companies, which shows the overall position of the group. It adds together all the assets and liabilities of the individual companies as shown by their respective balance sheets.

Naturally the inter-company balances have to be cancelled against each other. This is simple since each amount is an asset in one balance sheet and a liability in the other.

The share capital of each subsidiary cancels against the investment in that subsidiary shown as a parent company asset. If the subsidiary is not fully owned, the consolidated balance sheet will show, as a liability, the minority interest representing the shares not owned. If the parent company paid more for its investment than the nominal value of the shares, the premium is shown as goodwill in the consolidated balance sheet.

This is a simplified explanation of how a consolidated balance sheet is prepared. To look at, it is much the same as an ordinary balance sheet, the main difference being that if any subsidiaries are not fully owned or if an associate company's figures are consolidated the value of the outsiders' share of the group assets will be shown under the heading 'minority interest'.

What matters to creditors or lenders?

Since the consolidated balance sheet shows the overall position it tends to be given prominence and the parent company's balance sheet is often ignored by readers of accounts. However, this can be a mistake if you are a creditor or are lending money either to the parent company or to one of its subsidiaries.

The group, as consolidated, has no legal existence. It is the individual companies which one must sue in any dispute and, unless guarantees have been given, they are not responsible for each other's debts. It is usually impossible, legally speaking, to force a parent company to make good a deficiency in the assets of one of its subsidiaries.

It might be possible to realise the assets of a wholly owned subsidiary if you could force the parent into liquidation but it could be a long business if the subsidiary's directors were independent and reluctant to cooperate.

Remember that 51 per cent of a company is not enough to force a liquidation against the wishes of the other shareholders. Many consolidated balance sheets also include the assets of associated companies of which less than half the shares are owned. The creditors of the holding company are probably powerless to realise the assets of an associate company. Almost certainly their only possible course is to sell the shares and it might be very difficult to find a buyer for these unless they are quoted on the Stock Exchange.

So while consolidated balance sheets give vital information about the overall picture, they can be misleading if used to assess the security for a loan or an ordinary trading debt.

Look also at the parent company's figures (the holding company's balance sheet is published as well as the consolidated figures) or at those of the particular subsidiary with which you deal. Enquire for a parent company guarantee if in doubt.

What about income from associated companies?

If company A owns less than 50 per cent of company B, B is not a subsidiary but is often treated in the balance sheet of company A as an associated company, as explained in the previous chapter.

The significance of the 'associated company' heading is that the share of B's profits, which relates to the shares in it which A owns, is then brought in to A's consolidated accounts. This is in contrast to treating the income as being merely the actual dividend received.

One result of this is to show the group income as much larger than the amount over which the parent company's directors have direct control. They may not be able to force payment of a larger share of their associated company's profits and their own reported income may overstate the security available to a lender or creditor.

There is often a big difference between the dividend paid and the total profit applicable to a shareholding. This will depend upon the policy of the paying company, how much it needs to retain to pay for expansion plans and so on.

There have been many cases of companies holding valuable investments in other companies which were shown at a fraction of their true value, both because this was stated at a historic cost often many years old, and because the income shown ignored the profits retained by the paying company. Often it was difficult for outsiders to appreciate the facts for lack of detailed information. On the Stock Exchange this led to some unsatisfactory situations in which companies were taken over for prices vastly greater than their shares had been valued at on the basis of the published information available immediately before the take-over bid. The associated company method of accounting was therefore adopted in order to reflect the true position more closely but, as always, that 'truth' is not absolute. It can be misleading to a creditor.

Net assets per share

This is a figure often quoted in the financial press in connection with public companies. In the example, the calculation is:

	£
Shareholders' interest	209,000
Less preference shares	50,000
	£159,000
Divide by 45,000 = per share	£3.53

Questions

Check your answers with the text.
- What is the difference between a shareholder and a director?
- Why do shareholders need dividends?
- What is dividend cover?
- What is the difference between the balance sheet of a parent company and that of the whole group (ie the consolidated balance sheet)?

Chapter 9

What the Profit and Loss Account Tells You

Individual figures in your accounts mean little. It is in comparison with other figures that the key facts emerge.

Assessing your profits

Your profit and loss account shows you the result of your trading. Is it satisfactory?

Sales – did you sell more?

How much was the sales increase last year? Did it keep pace with inflation in the price of the goods or services you sell or did a rise in *money* totals, resulting from higher prices, conceal a fall in the *volume* of business?

Sales – how much could you have sold?

Is there a limit to your possible sales and, if so, how close did you get? If you are providing a service, you are really selling time. There may be skills and/or materials involved as well but it is time you are selling and there is only so much of it, unless you take on more staff. Once a service has sold enough hours to cover its fixed costs, every extra hour sold is profit subject only to materials and any other direct expenses. So a key factor in the profitability of a service is how close it gets to selling all its available time. On the other hand, once it is near to its maximum potential, it may only be able to increase sales by raising prices or taking on staff, which will increase costs – possibly more than sales.

Even a business selling goods may have an effective limit to its market. A shop on a housing estate normally can only hope to sell to people living on the estate. Their expenditure on any particular line of goods will be limited and the shop cannot hope for business beyond that limit.

These are simple examples but no business sells in a vacuum. What are the constraints on yours? How close are you to the effective limits to your volume of sales?

Are you making the right gross profit?

In Chapter 7 on the profit and loss account, I mentioned gross profit. Of all the key figures, this is the least understood, so here is some more on this important subject.

This is what gross profit means
Suppose you are a shopkeeper selling cakes at £2 each, which you buy at £1.50. You make a profit of 50p which is 25 per cent of the selling price. For simplicity, let's assume you sell only cakes.

If you dispose of 200 cakes a week, your gross profit is 25 per cent on sales of 200 × £2 = £400, ie £100 or 50p per cake. If the fixed costs of running your shop are £90 per week, you have a net profit of £10, or 5p per cake.

What happens to net profit if you raise your sales to 300 cakes per week? Stop here for a moment and work out for yourself, before reading on, how much your gross profit is and the net profit per cake.

300 cakes = sales £600 at 25 per cent = gross profit £150 (50p per cake) less fixed costs £90 = net profit £60 or 20p per cake. Your sales are up by half, gross profit has remained unchanged but net profit per cake has multiplied *four* times from 5p to 20p and the amount of net profit *six* times from £10 to £100!

The reason, of course, is that the fixed costs (wages, rent, rates, electricity etc) remain the same whether you sell one cake or 300. Perhaps a higher volume of sales creates a few more telephone calls or a little more wear and tear on fittings and equipment but such extra costs are insignificant. Of course, wages will rise when your existing staff can no longer cope but this will be a major jump owing to extra staff being taken on and will relate directly to the number of people you employ, not to the volume of sales as such, even though the latter is the cause.

Once you have paid your fixed costs, each extra cake sold produces 50p more net profit and that net profit spread over all the cakes sold rises dramatically until you have to engage extra staff.

Some cakes are wasted

Sadly, life is not so simple that that is the end of the story. Not every cake you buy gets sold. Here is why:

- Some are pushed to the back during busy sales periods and fresh stock goes in front by mistake, so the others go past their 'sell by' dates and have to be eaten by the owner or given to the staff.
- A few just fail to sell – the fillings, sizes etc – are not quite what customers want that week.
- Other cakes are spoilt in the window when the sun comes out unexpectedly and staff are too busy to erect the blind.
- Occasionally you guess the demand wrongly; perhaps the weather alters unexpectedly, there is a local scare about hygiene, another shop is prosecuted for selling cream cakes which are not fresh. Whatever the reason, it temporarily cuts sales and you find you have overbought.
- You deliver a large order to a local caterer and include an extra cake in error, or you price your invoice to him incorrectly, or you calculate the total wrongly.
- Your supplier short delivers you and you fail to check in time. Alternatively, he overcharges you per cake or makes a calculating error in his invoice which you do not spot. Occasionally he delivers the wrong cakes, too many cakes or substandard cakes and you do not discover these errors in time to claim credit. Some such mistakes by suppliers are genuine errors; others are deliberate fraud, often by staff of the supplier rather than the owner, as in the next example.
- You are busy when your supplier delivers and you do not notice the van driver removing one of the cartons which you have just hurriedly signed for. He sells it for cash elsewhere.
- One of your sales girls gives special prices to her friends without your knowledge or permission. A second assistant gets into financial trouble and starts to 'borrow' from the till. Another assistant has a sweet tooth and either eats on the premises or takes home cakes which are still fresh and in date. Customers pilfer a proportion of your stock.
- Your store room is crowded and you trip over a carton squashing it and sending another flying, rendering cakes in both cartons unsaleable.
- Your competitor down the road finds a new source of

cheaper supplies and he cuts prices, forcing you to follow suit.

- Some of your cakes sell by weight and there are minor but consistent undercharges to customers. Others are priced too low by mistake.

I hope your shop is not subject to such a catalogue of calamities all at once but there is no business which is free from all of them. Everyone has wastage of one kind or another. Whatever your trade or industry, you're bound to have similar problems.

The results of poor control of gross profit
Suppose that all the losses add up to just 1 per cent of the cakes you sell, ie three cakes on 300, value £6 at sale prices. Your figures are then:

	£
Sales: 297 at £2	594
Cost of goods sold: 300 at £1.50	450
(because you have to write off the missing 3 as well as the 297 sold)	
Gross profit	144
Net profit	£54

ie a reduction of 10 per cent from the previous profit of £60.

This level of loss may not seem too bad, but what if the losses are 3 per cent – nine cakes = £18 sales? The net profit is then down from £60 to £42, a fall of 30 per cent. That is quite a cut in your personal pay packet! And the dreadful reality is that 3 per cent of sales is on the low side for many businesses for pilferage losses, let alone all the others. Since many make less than 10 per cent of sales as net profit, you can see how serious this is.

Your gross profit is vital!
In the example of a profit and loss account in Chapter 4, gross profit (GP) has fallen from 24½ to 23 per cent. 1½ per cent on sales of £475,000 is £7,125. On the net profit of £15,800 this is 45.1 per cent. But one ought to compare it with the 'super'

profit of £1,400 on which it is 509 per cent! In fact this loss of GP is the main reason why the super profit has fallen and is so small in relation to the size of the business.

Small variations in GP often have a major impact upon the real profitability of the business. Usually it is easier to save 1 per cent of GP on sales than it is 10 per cent of an expense item. In the example given 1 per cent on sales is £4,750 which dwarfs the likely savings resulting from a blitz on expenses.

In retailing, similar shops start with roughly the same gross profit to play with. One supermarket's margins will be similar to another's; a small grocer buys on similar terms to other small grocers. As fixed expenses for equivalent shops are also similar, the main reason for the big differences in the net profit earned by comparable businesses is control of gross profit.

In non-retail businesses, other factors may play a bigger part but it is *always* true that the most effective way to raise profits is to tackle gross profit, because this is the largest figure which is susceptible to profit improvement.

Boosting sales is *not* an alternative; it could even make things worse by concentrating your attention on the wrong problems. Higher sales at lower prices do not necessarily mean more gross profit. Improving your cost of sales by better purchasing or more efficient use of materials or labour could be a more effective way of raising gross profit.

Let's look at it yet another way: to illustrate the arithmetic of wastage, consider what happens if you mark up the theoretical cost of your products by 33⅓ per cent. By theoretical cost, I mean what it should cost you to make an item, given normal usage of materials. A mark-up cost of 33⅓ per cent is the same as a margin on sales of 25 per cent. Thus £100 at cost becomes £133.33 of sales.

Suppose, however, that you have a wastage of materials in production of 5 per cent above the norm and loss of finished product owing to unsaleable goods or to pilferage, also of 5 per cent. Your cost becomes £105 instead of £100 while the sales proceeds fall from £133.33 to £126.67. Your gross profit is thus only £21.67 instead of £33.33. Instead of a gross margin of 25 per cent (£33.33 on £133.33), you earn 17.1 per cent (£21.67 on £126.67). Frightening, isn't it? That might be the whole of your net profit gone to waste.

Thus:

	Theoretical figures £		Actual figures £
Sales	400,000	down 5 %	380,000
Cost of sales	300,000	up 5 %	315,000
Gross profit 25 %	100,000	17.1 %	65,000
Overheads	65,000		65,000
Net profit 8.75 %	£35,000		£Nil

The business should be profitable. Instead it makes no money. Since waste goes with inefficiency generally, including in the book-keeping, the chances are that the owner's records aren't good enough to show the cause of the losses and that he has no idea where they are happening.

Whether or not my figures are typical in your case is not the point. Whatever your own situation, you will find that the potential impact of wastage on your gross profit dwarfs in importance every other daily consideration affecting the management of your money.

I'm not merely pontificating on the subject from the safety of a desk. I too have problems in minimising wastage of what I sell – my time. They are just different ones from those of a business handling goods. My message is that your gross profit margin deserves your best attention.

If you don't earn it gross, you can't have it net!

Factors which affect gross profit
Here are some of the key factors which affect how much gross profit you earn:

1. Wastage of all kinds: many of the causes have already been mentioned.
2. Pricing policy – low price/high volume or high price/low volume and discounts offered.
3. Skill in buying the right goods at the right price and in the right quantities.
4. Cash discounts obtained for prompt payment.
5. Manufacturing efficiency (if applicable), i.e:
   (a) effective use of materials
   (b) minimal machine downtime

(c) best use of production labour/efficient scheduling
(d) quality control.
6. Time charge-out ratios (for service industries and the professions)
    (a) ratio of hours charged out to those available from owners and staff
    (b) Control of work on own administration
    (c) control of sickness/absenteeism etc.

There are three important figures in your accounts, errors in which affect the gross profit.

1. *The stock valuation.* Obviously, if you have not counted and valued your stock accurately at the prices you paid, your gross profit will be distorted.
2. *Outstanding bills.* Your purchases figure, which is part of the cost of sales calculation, cannot be correct if you have not included all the invoices outstanding for goods you have used or counted in stock. See Chapter 7 if you are unclear about this.
3. *Sales on credit.* All deliveries to customers made prior to stock-taking must be invoiced if the sales figure is to be correct.

Analyse your gross profit
If your business sells different goods at widely differing profit margins, it pays to analyse your gross profit because an average will be meaningless. For example, a public house may have the following sales:

	Gross profit %	Sales £	Gross profit £
Bar	35	100,000	35,000
Wines	60	30,000	18,000
Food	60	80,000	48,000
Accommodation	N/A	50,000	50,000
	Average 58.1%	£260,000	£151,000

The *average* gross profit percentage, 58.1 per cent, is useless as a ratio for judging the results of the pub. It is made up of margins which vary widely and it is merely a statistic resulting from that particular sales mix. In order to assess the figures, it is necessary to look at them broken down by section of the business.

To illustrate this, suppose that the barman stole £200 per week, (£10,000 pa). In analysed accounts this would show up as a hole in the bar gross profit which would drop to only 27.8 per cent, ie £25,000 on £90,000. It would be evident that something was wrong.

If the figure was not analysed, the theft would reduce the overall gross profit to 56.4 per cent, ie £141,000 on £250,000. How could one spot the problem? Most likely it would go undetected because there would be no easy way of calculating what the gross profit ought to be.

So if your gross profits on different items vary widely, make sure you split your sales somehow. Even if you have to estimate the split using purchases grossed up by assumed profit margins, this is better than nothing.

Wages and salaries

Staff costs are always important though more so in some businesses than in others. In service industries, repair workshops and catering, for example, they tend to be vital because sales often depend upon the efficiency of the people who provide the service. Thus a café at peak periods can only improve its sales if customers are served more quickly.

Where labour itself is being sold, as in a repair workshop, the number of hours charged to customers, as a percentage of those paid for to staff, is a key ratio. Overtime hours worked may well be another.

After cost of sales, staff costs in most businesses are the largest expense and therefore offer the most scope for economy. It is good practice to put them at the top of the expenses list for this reason. Many sets of accounts hide the facts on staff costs by splitting them up under different headings; such analysis is often meaningless and merely conceals the size of this important figure.

Put all the elements which make up your staff costs together. Pension contributions, travel costs and car expenses are examples of items which are just as much a cost of employing people as their actual wages. They are usually shown as separate totals but should be listed together, not scattered haphazardly.

Other expenses

In some businesses, advertising and sales promotion costs, such as catalogues, brochures etc, are major items and need careful control in consequence.

The rest of your expenses are unlikely to matter very much. You need to know what they are and to keep track of how the totals are working out but some, such as rent and rates, can only be altered by moving premises. Few, if any, will be big enough to matter as much as gross profit and wages.

The telephone is one cost which does have to be watched more carefully; yet unless you have one of the sophisticated machines which record each call, it is difficult to keep any control on it at all.

Here's a tip which at least will help you to see what is happening. Your telephone bill is made up of three elements: a standing charge, the number of units used and the price per unit. Keep a special record of your bills showing each of these elements plus the total of the bill. Then you will be able to see whether the key one, the number of units, is going up. Higher bills could be because of changes in the standing charges or the price per unit. It's the usage you need to check on and a record kept over a couple of years is helpful in showing the pattern of what is happening.

Concentrate on your key figures

In most businesses there are only two or three figures which have a major impact on profits and which also change daily or weekly. They are usually sales, gross profit margins, wages (or staff use) and perhaps one other, depending on the business. These four items have a far greater impact than all the other details put together.

Go through your detailed costs once or twice a year to see if you can cut out items, stop using this or that service, simplify equipment such as telephones, improve heating efficiency etc. Then leave them alone and concentrate on the things you can change day by day, where improvements can yield really big benefits.

Figures as a percentage of sales

Since only the gross profit varies directly with sales, this is the most useful profit and loss ratio.

Staff costs as a percentage of annual sales over a period of years may be significant because it can reveal trends. To control staff costs, however, one must refer to numbers employed, pay rises negotiated etc.

In some cases advertising and promotion are a big cost which requires highlighting as a percentage of sales, because average industry ratios are a useful comparison with the competition.

Most of the other expenses of a business are either not big enough in relation to GP and wages to matter, or are fixed. Other expense percentages, therefore, are not usually key ratios and it is pointless to calculate them.

Net profit percentage on sales

This is a useful guide to the progress of a business over a period of years. Sometimes it is a valid comparison between businesses in the same trade. However, its value is as a relative figure in comparison with others. Absolute percentage profits on sales vary enormously. Even in the same trade, different businesses may have quite different methods of operation. One may process customers' materials while another supplies its own. The sales totals will be different to achieve the same net profit.

Net profit expressed as return on net capital employed is a key ratio which is dealt with under balance sheet key ratios.

Do not misuse ratios

In the example of the net profits per cake quoted earlier, the rise from 5p to 20p per cake was interesting, exciting, big news. But what did it actually tell you about the business other than that profits were improving fast? Nothing, because the ratio, as a basis for management action, is meaningless and is of interest only as an annual trend indicator. Many people who ought to know better waste their own and others' time on ratios which are either meaningless or misleading in terms of day-to-day management.

Some managers (some accountants too) regard ratios as an end in themselves, regardless of what useful action may result. They insist on calculating them and they use the figures which are readily available, whether or not these are comparable or relevant, and without troubling to ask themselves why. The effect on the morale of their subordinates or colleagues, who know the results to be useless but who are expected to respond to or explain them, can be disastrous. Might you be guilty?

Questions

Check your answers with the text.

- Which are the key ratios in the example given and discussed above?
- Which are the key ratios in your own business?
- Why are they relevant and why do they matter?

Chapter 10

What the Balance Sheet Tells You

As with the profit and loss account, the balance sheet will only tell you the right story if you understand how the figures relate to each other. Ratios are often more revealing than the figures on which they are based.

This chapter explains various terms which need to be understood because there are no simple substitutes for them. Besides, if you want the best out of your accountant, it helps to be able to talk his language.

Are the figures typical?

The balance sheet only gives figures at one date. This may or may not be typical – many financial year ends are at quiet periods to ease stock-taking etc.

When considering balance sheet ratios, therefore:
1. Consider whether the figures used reflect the normal position.
2. Use the correct figures which relate to each other; thus debtor balances relate to sales immediately prior to the balance sheet date, not to the average for the whole period. Also they include value added tax (VAT), unlike the sales figure, so to compare the two, one must add the VAT on to the sales total, if it applies.

Note: The figures in this chapter use the balance sheet in Chapter 5.

Capital employed

The total funds in use by the business, ie the total of its assets. In the example this is £133,800.

Net capital employed

Total assets less current liabilities, except the bank overdraft. Current liabilities, principally creditors, are in effect finance provided by outsiders for short periods. Thus the net capital which the owner has to provide is reduced by the normal trade credit he receives. The overdraft, in contrast, is a method of financing part of his cash needs and does not arise automatically from trading. Therefore it should not reduce the net capital employed figure which in the example is £133,800 − £19,000 = £114,800.

An important measure of the profitability of the business is the return earned upon net capital employed; see page 80.

Working capital

The cash required to operate the business from day to day, ie to pay for stocks, debtors, advance payments to creditors, deposits etc. The amount is reduced by creditors, advance payments from customers etc. Thus current assets less current liabilities represents at the date of the balance sheet the working capital in use by the business. Any bank overdraft should be added back to the net balance for the reason explained above under net capital employed. It is more realistic to regard it as a means of funding than as part of working capital.

Net capital employed and working capital

The respective figures from the example are set out to show how the two terms differ.

	Net capital employed £	Working capital £
Fixed assets and goodwill	55,800	N/A
Current assets	78,000	78,000
	133,800	78,000
Less current liabilities except bank overdraft	19,000	19,000
Net capital employed/working capital	114,800	59,000
Funded by:		
the bank	34,000	34,000
the owner	60,800	25,000
long-term loan	20,000	N/A
	£114.800	£59,000

In this case the bank is providing 58 per cent of the net working capital, which is all right but the bank might not wish the proportion to go higher. See also under balance sheet ratios.

Too high a proportion of bank finance is often a sign of overtrading. This occurs when sales expand beyond the capacity of the business to provide the necessary working capital for stock and debtors – hence increased borrowings.

Current assets to current liabilities

This is an important test. The right ratio varies from trade to trade and with the nature of the assets. In retailing one might be happy with anything over 1.25:1 because stocks, correctly managed, are fairly easily cleared and are often largely funded by creditors.

In manufacturing stocks have to be held longer and in various stages of production so that one cannot rely as much upon credit. A ratio of at least 1.5:1 is desirable.

In the example it is £78,000 to £53,200 or 1.5 (last year 1.4).

Another factor in judging a particular situation is the extent to which the bank is financing current assets. An overdraft, being repayable upon demand, is not the same as normal trade credit, which will continue so long as the trade reputation of the business is good.

Properly managed businesses keep their current ratios in line. A ratio which is below average for the particular trade is a sign of one or more faults:

(a) losses eroding cash.
(b) bad cash planning – using short-term money to pay for fixed assets or to fund long-term projects.

While an above average current ratio may reflect financial strength, it may also suggest idle cash and a business which is not fully exploiting its resources.

Liquidity – the acid test

This is a more severe test of the ability of the business to pay its debts, sometimes called the 'acid test'. It is the ratio of quick assets – those current assets which can quickly be turned into cash – to current liabilities.

In the example, debtors of £10,700 compare with current

liabilities of £53,200. Stocks do not count as quick assets because, in most cases, only a part of them could be realised quickly. Often that part of stocks which is saleable at once is matched by debtors from whom rapid payment is not obtainable.

The seriousness of the position in the example depends upon when the tax is payable and upon the attitude of the bank. Should it put on pressure for a reduction in the overdraft this could only come from cutting stocks.

In the example, the business has an overdraft. Naturally, if there is cash in the bank, this counts as part of quick assets.

Debtors to sales

This is debtors including VAT compared with sales after adding back VAT. The correct ratio is that of debtors to sales for the weeks immediately prior to the date of the balance sheet, *not* debtors to the average of the annual sales. Naturally, where sales fluctuate in the course of a year, more detail is required than is shown in the profit and loss account.

In the example little credit is given and debtors are just over a week's sales, assuming VAT at 15 per cent; ie

$$\frac{£475,000 + 15\%}{52} = \begin{array}{l}\text{Sales £105,000 per week compared with} \\ \text{debtors of £10,700}\end{array}$$

The ratio indicates whether a proper credit control policy is in force. The correct number of days outstanding varies, of course, according to the credit terms you offer your customers.

Stocks to usage (cost of sales)

Again the stocks at the balance sheet date are often low in comparison with the average so that the ratio requires enquiry before acceptance as valid. Also not all stocks shown necessarily relate to cost of sales. Some may be stationery, fuel or other expense items.

In the example, trade stocks of £65,000 against usage (cost of sales) £365,600 or £7,030 weekly suggests 9.2 weeks' usage held (last year £5,990 per week = 8.7 weeks). This might be reasonable for a manufacturer or retailer working on high profit margins, but would be too high for a grocer, for example, whose stocks should be fast moving because they are perishable and on low margins. But is the June stock figure representative?

In the case of a manufacturer, cost of sales might include some labour and other production costs; so might the stock valuation so check before accepting the ratio. Labour and other costs must be in both the figures used in calculating the ratio or not at all.

The stocks ratio indicates the effectiveness of the control of buying, skill in forecasting sales, the efficiency of the stockroom and, where applicable, the efficiency in production. It is vitally important. Bad stock control ties up both cash and space. It causes stock losses through damage, excess quantities etc, and makes it more difficult to bring in new lines, change policy to meet new conditions, etc.

Creditors to purchases and expenses

Recent purchases may not be typical. As an example, a build-up of stocks for Christmas might invalidate a ratio of average purchases during the year to creditors at 30 November. To see the true picture you would need the purchases for the weeks prior to that date, not the annual average.

Remember that creditors include VAT but purchases do not.

In the example, purchases are £378,600 and expenses about £33,000, ignoring wages and rent which are not incurred on credit. Adding VAT at 15 per cent, the total is £473,340, or about £9,100 weekly average. Less than two weeks' credit suggests a failure to use normal trade terms. If prompt payment is being made to obtain cash discounts, why has the gross profit ratio fallen? Or is the June creditors total not representative?

The ratio indicates the extent to which creditors are paid promptly. This has various implications concerning reputation, discounts obtained etc.

Net profits to net capital employed

In the example, net capital employed is £133,800 − £19,000 = £114,800. Adding back interest on the overdraft and loan of £7,000 gives a profit of £22,800 or 19.9 per cent (last year £21,000 on £107,800 = 19.5 per cent). This is well ahead of the interest cost on the money borrowed.

Super profit to proprietor's interest

But look at this ratio: super profit of £1,400 on the owner's interest of £60,600 is about 2.3 per cent. If the calculation is adjusted for interest and loans the figures are £8,400 on £114,800 = 7.3 per cent (last year £7,900 on £107,800 = 7.3 per cent). In recent years one has often been able to earn as much or more simply by leaving one's money in a bank!

The calculation of true profit, ie after charging a working wage for the owner as a percentage of his interest in the business, is often a salutary exercise.

You must aim to earn a premium over the return obtainable from selling the business, taking a job and investing the cash. Otherwise why bother with the extra effort and responsibility and the longer working hours?

Equally, if expansion is planned, the cash borrowed, or realised from investments, to pay for it must earn a profit in excess of its interest cost.

Suppose your current super profit on net capital employed is 17.5 per cent on £50,400. This should not necessarily rule out borrowing money at, say, 20 per cent. If, for example, £12,000 could be borrowed at 20 per cent for a project which would generate extra sales of £40,000 at a gross profit of 23 per cent without extra staff or other significant expenses, the result would be as follows:

	Super profit before interest £	Net capital employed £	Percentage return %
Current	8,800	50,400	17.5
New sales £40,000 at 23% GP = extra profit	9,200		
Cash borrowed at 20 % interest cost	(2,400)	12,000	
New result	£15,600	£62,400	25.0

While it may be optimistic to suggest a sales increase of £40,000 without increasing overheads, it does illustrate how figures need to be seen in perspective, not in isolation.

In this example, the current figures might reflect under-use of assets and staff which is remedied by the new project even though the money costs 20 per cent. Hence all the extra gross profit comes through as net profit.

Questions

Check your answers with the text.

- What is:
  - capital employed?
  - net capital employed?
  - working capital?
- What are the seven ratios mentioned above?
- In what form is each expressed?

Chapter 11
How Cash Circulates in a Business

Why do cash ratios matter?

Many of the key business ratios previously explained reveal the efficiency with which cash is used. A business can get away with bad cash use reflected in poor liquidity, high debtors, stocks and creditors, heavy overdrafts etc provided its profitability is high. But as soon as anything goes wrong, its cash shortage puts it at risk. Any loss of confidence by its creditors squeezes it hard. A business which is basically profitable but which mis-manages its cash can easily be toppled by a temporary setback into liquidation because it has no room to manoeuvre.

A basic rule of cash management

Fixed assets and long-term development should by financed by retained profits or by loans on fixed repayment terms. That way one can plan for repayment of the cash out of profits.

Bank overdrafts are only suitable for financing current assets such as debtors and stock. Being repayable on demand, they should only be invested in assets which can be realised quickly. Otherwise you are in the dangerous position of investing long and borrowing short.

Cash is your lifeblood!

Businesses go bust for lack of cash, not necessarily because they are not making profits. What actually breaks them is inability to pay their bills.

The water tank chart

How well does your business use its money? Efficient cash control is vital to stability and profits. Perhaps you realise that your equipment, stocks and amounts owed by customers are 'money' to be controlled, just like your bank balance, but do your colleagues or your employees?

An understanding of how cash circulates in a business is important not only for the boss but for the staff too. Even in the smaller business, the boss needs the cooperation of employees if the amount of cash tied up is to be minimised. My tank chart on page 85 is especially valuable in getting the idea across to non-accountants because it explains it in physical terms.

The chart shows, in engineers' language, how a business uses money. Cash circulates like water which flows through a system of tanks, partly by gravity and partly through a pump.

Where does the money come from?

At the start of the business the owner(s) provide loans or pay up share capital; the bank may make a loan or provide an overdraft facility. This finance flows into the bank account and it's all the money there is. It can't come from anywhere else.

Gravity feed

It's easy to spend money. From the bank account cash flows out at the turn of a tap, so to speak, into fixed assets and stocks. Some is lost as stock wastage. A little comes back when assets are sold off.

In some businesses, there ought to be an extra tank for research and development costs carried forward in the balance sheet because they relate to new products not yet launched. It's all too easy to sink cash into R and D.

Perhaps less readily, cash is then absorbed in giving credit for sales. Some leaks away as bad debts. How much each tank absorbs depends on how you run your business.

The gross profit margin

The cost in cash of a sale is what you have spent in producing the item or providing the service. To that cost is added your profit margin to make the amount owing by the customer which is shown in your balance sheet. This profit inflates the debtors' tank, but is not yet cash in hand.

The pump house gets the money back in

From then on cash only flows back up round the system when

How cash circulates in a business

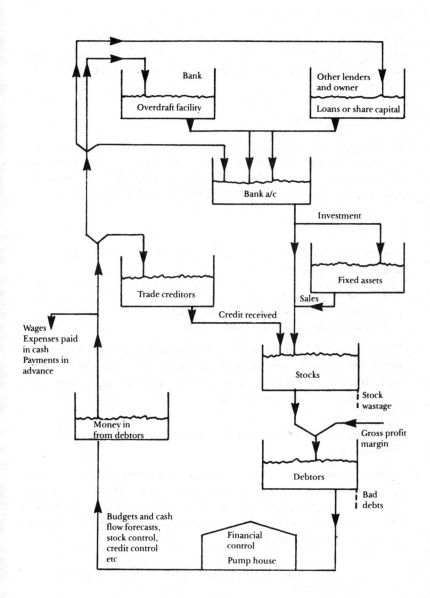

pumped via the financial control pump house which is powered by budgets, cash flow forecasts, stock control etc.

Money in from debtors

This is a temporary holding tank included to emphasise how sales are only cash once debts are collected. From this tank payments are made for cash expenses and the other tanks are refilled.

Trade credit tank

If you pay your suppliers regularly, the trade credit tank will continue its gravity feed which finances stocks. But should an interruption in supply from 'Money in from debtors' occur, it will quickly run dry as creditors withdraw facilities.

Bank account

Finally, the bank account tank is replenished. This has three sources of supply:

1. retained profit
2. owner's capital (in share or loans)
3. bank overdraft or other loans.

Both the owner's and the bank's tanks need periodic replenishment if they are to be able and willing to continue providing the extra finance which is needed as inflation raises stock values etc, let alone to pay for expansion.

Too much cash in one tank reduces the cash available elsewhere

Since the cash supply in the business is limited, an excess in one tank must drain off from another, perhaps causing a shortage. The excess may be caused by poor control of spending decisions or by failure to collect debts. This reflects itself in the various ratios previously discussed.

What are the financial decisions made in your organisation? Who takes them?

These are catch questions to see whether the previous message has sunk in! Before continuing, consider how the money is spent in your business and who takes the decisions. Refer back to the water tank chart when working out your answers and write them down here under the headings:

Decisions to spend.
Who takes them?

The decisions are made thus

The decision to spend is irrevocable once the order is placed for an asset, such as a piece of equipment, a vehicle etc, or for goods or materials for resale or use in manufacture. Once a sale is made on credit to a customer, cash has been committed to that deal.

These are the points at which the commitment is made. The subsequent payment is inevitable sooner or later. Cash management must therefore start with control over the placing of orders. The management of the accounts payable (creditors) ledger, or invoices outstanding, can be helpful, particularly in squeezing a little extra credit when money is particularly tight, but it is really only tinkering with the problem. Once the order is placed it is usually too late to avert the need to make the payment.

The third decision point, that of granting credit to customers, is not the same as the others. No actual payment is made; on the contrary, money is subsequently received from the customer. Nevertheless, there is a cost of granting credit. This is not just the interest charges on the money which is outstanding. Every time goods go out of the business on credit, they have to be replaced by other goods in order to maintain stocks. Frequently it is not the production manager or the buyer who causes an order for goods or materials in the first place, but the sales manager who creates the need to buy in further supplies by making the credit sale in the first place.

Whether these jobs are all done by one man or by a team of people, it is important to understand how the different decisions interlock with each other.

I don't want to overstress the spending of money by the sales manager when he grants credit. His job, after all, is to obtain sales. However, he should understand that the responsibility for operating the company's credit policy starts with him and that this is not just red tape for the benefit of the accounts department.

The arithmetic of credit control

Do you understand the arithmetic involved in a bad debt? If your gross profit is 30 per cent you have materials and direct expenses, value £70, in a £100 bad debt. To recover that loss of £70, you will therefore need to make a further £230 of sales. This is bad enough, but consider the situation if you take the net profit on the sale. Since the collection of the money from the customer is the last operation in the whole chain of events, it is reasonable to charge to a sale more than just the direct cost of producing the goods or the services. After paying all the over-heads, salaries etc of the business, many net profits are no more than 10 per cent or less of the sales value. To recover the real loss on a bad debt of £100 at a net profit margin of 10 per cent, ie £90, you will need to make no less than £900 of new sales.

Even if you argue that this overstates the case because the administrative and other overhead costs will not increase in proportion to the extra sales required to recover the bad debt, the true increase in sales needed to cover the bad debt must surely lie at least halfway between the two figures, ie around £500 to £600.

The executive team

I hope that I have now persuaded you that the financial decisions in your business are not taken by just one person. It is the entire executive team which is involved.

Even in the smallest organisations this is true. The small shopkeeper does not have executives as such, but his staff are, or should be, involved in taking stock and keeping track of goods required etc. If you have not managed to involve your staff so that they understand the importance of minimising stocks and of having the right goods to hand to meet customers' requirements, if they do not take an active part in helping you to achieve those objectives, you are not running your business at its maximum effectiveness.

In the larger organisation, the team may consist of one or more of the following executive staff:

Buyer
Production manager
Development manager
Research manager
Despatch manager
Head storeman
Sales manager
and, of course, the Boss.

Why the research manager?

This applies only to those readers whose businesses spend a significant sum of money each year on research and development (R and D) of one kind or another. These businesses should have a subheading or division of the fixed assets tank in the water tank chart between fixed assets and research and development.

Research and development is a tank of enormous size into which huge sums can flow with no resulting value whatever.

The problem of R and D is always to make it start producing cash. This is not a matter of 'as quickly as possible', so much as 'within reasonable time'. The scientist or technician always wants to perfect his product before putting it on the market. This is in direct conflict with the need of the organisation, which is to get some cash coming in to offset the continuing expenditure. If R and D produces a product, which generates cash to pay for the continuing cost of improving it, it is valuable to the company. On the other hand, R and D which simply absorbs cash over an indefinite period in large amounts may very well destroy it. However good the potential, however technically exciting the project, future possibilities have never paid current bills.

Are your priorities muddled?

Cash is 'spent' by the people who order things or who grant credit to customers, not when cheques are signed. Often orders, particularly for stock items, are initiated by junior staff who are unaware of policy decisions on product development, discontinuation of lines etc. Resulting mistakes can tie up money in surplus or unusable stocks.

Say a clerk orders 10,000 units of a component for a product of which you have been selling 2,000 a month but which is due to be phased out shortly. The financial loss will not only be the useless stock which no one wants, even for scrap; by the time the problem is identified, the components will have taken up expensive space in your stockroom, got in the way of the efficient running of your stores and occupied people's time to check them in etc. The consequent inefficiency may have cost as much as the direct loss.

Orders for stock from suppliers merit the attention of senior management. Yet they rarely get it. It is often not them but the purchase of a typewriter which requires the approval of the managing director. The potential loss is small; his secretary understands typewriters better and, even if she gets it wrong, the machine can be sold quickly at a limited loss. How many muddled priorities like this are there in your organisation?

What about your own priorities?

If, as the boss or the financial director, you spend your time pushing paper on relatively trivial matters because they are easy to pin down instead of on those aspects of the business of fundamental importance financially, you can hardly expect your staff or your colleagues not to copy you.

You must delegate effectively. That means persuading your staff to take responsibility for detail and, if you employ managers, they too must delegate in the same way. People down the line of authority won't handle responsibility well, however, unless they understand why. Hence the importance of using the tank chart to explain why the details matter: details like those computer statements we all get, which are obviously wrong and which provide the perfect excuse not to pay – the 'system' just sends them out, when a quick check by staff would pick up the errors; details like that despatch note not yet passed for invoicing, which represents money owed by a customer who won't pay until he gets his bill; or the pile of goods, stuck in the wrong place and hidden behind other stock, which is urgently needed on the production line and represents cash which the business can't ask for until the order goes out. Explaining could make all the difference to the way staff take responsibility for the detail in your organisation.

To summarise

Cash disappears easily into fixed assets, stocks and debtors. It only comes back when customers pay. To make sure they pay and to keep to a minimum the money you need to run the business, you must exercise financial control.

Cash is scarce. Conserving it should be the concern of everyone who works in the business. That means telling people why it matters and how they can help. The tank chart is a good way of doing this because it sets the matter out in a way which people find easy to understand. Are you sure *you* understand? Try filling in the blank chart on page 92 now.

How cash circulates in a business

Exercise: Fill in descriptions in the correct places. They are listed at the bottom of the chart.

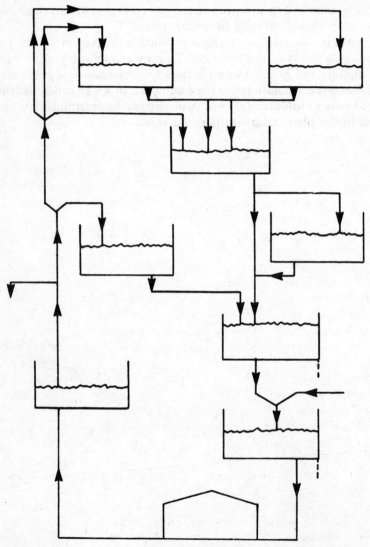

Debtors	Bank: Overdraft facility	Money in from debtors
Trade creditors	Actual account	Stock wastage
Fixed assets	Bad debts	Pump house
Stocks	Wages and other cash expenses	Owner and lenders
		Gross profit margin

Chapter 12

What the Statement of Source and Application of Cash Tells You

In Chapter 11, we saw how cash circulates in a business. Chapter 1, pointed out that inability to pay its bills puts a business out of business and that controlling your cash is just as important as making a profit. Now I'll explain what I call the statement of source and application of cash.

Up to now, I have said that a set of accounts consists only of the profit and loss account and the balance sheet. These are indeed the two main documents but, although they show whether or not a profit has been earned and what the state of the business is at the end of its financial year, they do not show clearly what has happened to the cash. They do not explain how the profit relates to the bank balance.

Since it is possible to earn a good profit and yet find oneself even deeper into the red, this is important. It is the statement of source and application of cash which forms the missing link. It shows how cash has been generated by or used up in the business. It starts with the profit for the year, as stated by the profit and loss account, and ends with the bank balance shown in the balance sheet.

Well, at least it ought to! I'm afraid that accountants often obscure the message by calling it the source and application of *funds*, not *cash*. They use a different layout from the one I illustrate so you may not recognise my version from the one you will find in most annual accounts.

Professors of accounting theory would say that my *cash* statement oversimplifies the situation for a big company. They are welcome to use statements of source and application of funds which may well be more appropriate for major public companies. For the practical businessman, especially in the smaller company, I contend that they are useless because they not only use incomprehensible jargon but they fail to link the profit to the bank balance clearly.

To see what I mean, I suggest you look at my example on page 94 and compare it with the one in your own accounts. You

Example of a statement of source and application of cash
(Figures in brackets are cash outflows or overdrafts)

Source of cash	£
Profit for the year before tax	15,800
Add depreciation	10,000
Loss on disposal of fixed asset	200
Total from trading	26,000
Sale of fixed assets	—
Loan received	—
Total cash available	26,000

Application of cash

Payments not chargeable against profits

Fixed assets bought (capital expenditure)	(6,000)
Tax paid on profits	(2,500)
Owner's drawings	(10,000)
Net cash left in the business	7,500

Changes in working capital
Current assets:

Stocks	(Increase) Decrease	(13,000)
Debtors	(Increase) Decrease	(1,000)
Payments in advance	(Increase) Decrease	(200)

Current liabilities:

Creditors	Increase (Decrease)	2,500
Advance payments by customers	Increase (Decrease)	—
Cash (used for) or released from working capital		(11,700)

Net increase or (decrease) during year in cash held	(4,200)
Opening cash balance (overdraft)	(30,000)
Closing cash balance (overdraft)	(£34,200)

may find that the statement does not end with the balance in the bank account but with some other total. I find this meaningless. If you do too, try reorganising the figures so that they fit into my layout.

You may then find that they make some sense and that they show you clearly what has happened to your money. If you decide you prefer a *cash* statement like mine, I suggest you ask your accountant to produce it. They are your accounts not his, so you are entitled to insist on this.

My example uses the figures for the XYZ shop in Chapters 4 and 5.

Source of cash

We start with the profit for the year before tax from the profit and loss account. We add to it the depreciation for the year. There are two figures for depreciation in the profit and loss account which relate to equipment, fixtures and fittings and to a motor vehicle and the total is £10,000.

The reason why we add depreciation back to the profit, when considering cash flow, is that the figure doesn't represent an actual payment. Money was paid for the assets when they were bought and they are now being written off by depreciation, the latter representing an amount set aside from the profit. If you are unclear about this, see the section on depreciation on page 32.

You may find that your profit and loss account shows either a profit or a loss on the sale of a fixed asset. If it does, you must adjust the profit for the year before tax by deducting the fixed asset profit – or adding back the loss. The reason is that a fixed asset profit or loss is the difference between the book value and the money received. It is not the cash itself.

Now we put in the actual money received on the sale of fixed assets line. That figure will not be shown in either the profit and loss account or the balance sheet though you may be able to work it out if the book value of the fixed assets written off is shown, since the cash received must be the book value plus a profit or minus a loss. If not, it will have to come from your detailed records.

In the example, there is no figure to put in because the £200 disposal is not a sale; it is the value of an item which has been scrapped. Some accountants use the word 'retirements' to mean assets taken out of use which are either scrapped or sold, though I regard 'retirements' as more cumbersome and no clearer than 'disposal'.

For loans, you must look at the balance sheet example in the section which follows the one on the profit and loss account. Since the loan has not changed during the year, there has been no cash received and there is nothing to enter.

This means that the total cash available is £26,000.

Application of cash

The lower part of the form then explains how the cash generated by trading was used.

Figures in brackets are minuses
The figures shown in brackets are outflows of cash. Thus fixed assets bought is a payment. An increase in stocks also represents an outflow because money has had to be paid to finance that increase. A reduction in debtors represents an inflow and is not in brackets because it means that customers have paid up more promptly so that cash is in the bank instead of being tied up in debtors.

For creditors, the position is the other way round. An increase in creditors means that the latter are lending money on short-term credit to the business. A reduction in creditors means that they have been paid more promptly and there is a corresponding outflow from the bank account.

Payments not chargeable against profits

These figures come from the balance sheet. Your own balance sheet may show the value of the fixed assets bought during the year but, if not, you will find the figure in the attached note on fixed assets. Here it is shown on the face of the balance sheet and the figure is £6,000.

The tax paid on profits is the figure relating to the previous year, not the provision for tax on this year's profits which will not be due until next year. Tax is payable in arrears because it cannot be worked out until the profit is known.

The figure for owner's drawings comes from the balance sheet too. For a limited company, the equivalent is the dividends paid on the share capital and the figure is not shown in the accounts. It has to be worked out from the information they give. During each year, the amount paid is the final dividend for the previous year plus an interim one for the current year – assuming that there is an interim dividend. The final dividend can only be paid after the end of the year because it has first to be approved at the annual general meeting of the company.

Changes in working capital

As explained above and in Chapter 11, changes in stocks, debtors, creditors etc either absorb cash or release it. As a business grows, it needs more cash to finance stocks and debtors because higher sales require bigger stocks and larger debtors. Some of the cash is provided by creditors who supply the stocks on credit. Usually, however, the business cannot sell its stocks and collect the money from its customers quickly enough to pay all its creditors on time so it needs extra working capital finance in order to grow.

Alternatively, in a badly managed business, stock and debtors may rise simply because they are not properly controlled.

Here, the figures shown come from the balance sheet and you can see how I get to them by comparing the 'last year' and 'this year' figures.

As there are no advance payments by customers in this particular balance sheet, there is no entry on that line.

The various minus figures in brackets and the plus figure for finance provided by creditors net to a minus figure in the next line representing cash used for working capital.

Then we compare that minus total with the figure for net cash left in the business on the line higher up and find there is a net decrease in cash held during the year of £4,200. The balance sheet tells us that the starting bank overdraft was £30,000 as shown in the last year column. This enables us to calculate the closing bank overdraft as £34,200. As this agrees with the figure in the balance sheet, the arithmetic is correct.

Thus, the statement of source and application of cash has reconciled the profit from the profit and loss account with the change in the bank balance.

Chapter 13

How to Get a Grip on Your Cash Position – Now

Is keeping track of your day-to-day cash balance a problem for you? Would you like an immediate feel for the cash position of your business? The cash flow report can give it to you. It's one of the most valuable – perhaps the most important – control documents any business can have.

Do you have answers to these questions at your fingertips?

How much money can you expect to come in over the next month?
How much will you have to pay out?
Where will this leave your bank balance or overdraft?
Will you have enough cash to keep your creditors at bay or will you need to borrow?
What is today's bank balance and is there spare cash at the moment which could go on deposit to earn interest for a week or two?
Will you be able to pay the PAYE/NI contributions and VAT on time?
What are the totals now of your debtors and creditors (accounts receivable and accounts payable)?

If you cannot answer these questions quickly, you do not know enough about your cash flow. You are running the money side of the your business blind. This leads to crisis management in which time and energy are wasted in coping with short-term cash problems instead of earning profit.

My cash flow report is the answer. This chapter shows you how to use it to get a grip immediately on the short-term cash situation of any business, whatever its size. I have never seen such a report anywhere else, though I am sure others must have had the same idea. It is a simple document which I developed in a situation of dire necessity when, for two and a half years, I ran the finances of a company which was making losses and which was in danger of liquidation throughout that period.

The report did not remedy our long-term financial problems

but it enabled me to cope with the short-term results of them. It helped me so to manage our meagre resources that we never had a supplier either cut off supplies or refuse us normal trade credit. It showed me how quickly our customers were paying us and I also used it to decide for how much I could authorise my purchase ledger clerk to write cheques to our suppliers each week.

It also showed me what bills were looming up for payment, such as the monthly PAYE/NI contributions and the quarterly VAT. Having the report meant I could not only manage the cash week by week but I could also forecast, one to two months ahead, what our overdraft would be. Not only did we never exceed our limit as a result, in spite of frightful trading difficulties, but I was even able to earn useful interest on short-term deposits for the occasional periods when we had funds in hand, because I knew for how long I could lend the money out.

Two versions of the report are shown: the first is a simplified one suitable for small businesses, especially those which sell services rather than goods. The second is for larger concerns and those which buy goods for resale.

I use the small business version in my consultancy business. It tells me most of the key financial facts of my affairs every Monday morning including my sales, debtors (accounts receivable), expenses and bank balance. It helps me earn extra interest on money, which I put on deposit more quickly because I have the figures at my fingertips each week. It stops me running into an overdraft at the bank unnecessarily by writing cheques for more than the current balance.

It must be the same in your business. If you haven't got a regular report showing the bank balance, it takes much faffing about to find the paying-in and cheque books and work out a rough one – which tends to be wrong anyway. Somehow, one always needs to know quickly. This report saves me a great deal of time and worry working out whether the money is there when I want to pay a bill. Just how much it had become a part of my way of working and how lost I would be without it I realised when I moved my house and office. With the problems of the move and recruiting a new secretary, my cash flow report slipped for several weeks. I felt financially blind.

The beauty of the report is that it is simple. You'll probably need to adapt my layout to suit your business but, once you've set it up, anyone can extract the figures from your records for you. All they need is common sense, a calculator or, better still, an add/listing machine and access to your sales invoices or sales daybook, if you keep one, your paying-in book and your cheque book. As a bonus, the report will even give you the output figures you need for the dreaded VAT return - so that's part of another problem solved as well!

The main point of the report, however, is to help you manage your money. Whether you need to spin out meagre resources, as I had to in my earlier job, or to earn the maximum interest on spare funds, it will help you too to manage your finances better.

You can produce your first cash flow report today. Once you have got it going, it should not take more than half an hour to do each week, less with practice, especially in a small business. All the figures are available now in your records, however sketchy your accounting system may be, so this powerful tool is yours for the asking.

If you already have a budget for your business, note that the report is not a substitute for an annual cash flow forecast. The latter estimates for a year ahead the cash position month by month on the basis of the budgeted sales and expenses. The cash flow report, on the other hand, works from the actual figures as they happen. Its role is to enable you to control the position week by week. The actual totals can then be compared with the budgeted ones to enable you to see how close you will be to the latter.

An example of a simple cash flow report

This is the version of the report which I use myself. It is suitable for any service business, ie one which sells time rather than goods, though it may need adapting to suit your precise circumstances. It is intended for those who do not have a full double entry accounting system. If you do, or if you hold stocks of goods for resale, you will probably find the second version on page 108 more suitable but I suggest you skim through this in order to see the general idea.

I round all my figures to the nearest pound except for the VAT. This has to be precise because it is tax due to the government. By including the pence, I can use the weekly totals to give me the quarterly output tax total I need for my VAT return. I do not need pence for the output figure itself - there is no

A simple cash flow report

	Line	Week 40 £	Week 41 £	Week 42 £	Week 43 £	Cumulative position £
Opening debtors	1	8,248	10,756	10,357	8,975	7,967
Invoiced: Consultancy	2	1,464	791	2,990	210	27,855
Seminars	3	118	—	—	—	6,682
Writing	4	1,416	—	—	—	4,469
Subtotal; SR sales	5	2,998	791	2,990	210	39,006
Travel	6	—	50	120	—	2,290
Motor	7	40	—	—	—	420
Telephone	8	25	15	31	8	550
Subtotal; SR outputs	9	3,063	856	3,141	218	42,266
Books ZR	10	105	70	99	105	1,363
Total outputs	11	3,168	926	3,240	323	43,629
VAT	12	459.45	128.40	471.15	32.70	6,340
Total invoiced	13	3,627	1,054	3,711	355	49,969
Less closing debtors	14	10,756	10,357	8,975	7,887	7,887
Money in	15	1,119	1,453	5,093	1,443	50,049
Money out						
Wages/PAYE and NI	16	210			2,337	26,289
Rent	17	54				1,164
Telephone	18					705
Travel	19	95			89	691
Motor	20	79				553
Petty cash	21			79		802
Sundry	22	46			220	1,092
SOs and bank charges	23		2			90
Subtotal; expenses	24	484	2	79	2,646	31,386
Capital expenditure	25		1,500			1,823
Income/corp tax	26				500	500
Drawings	27	20				2,885
VAT paid to C&E	28				1,850	5,218
Deposit account	29				2,000	8,595
Total paid out	30	504	1,502	79	6,996	50,407
Net cash flow	31	615	(49)	5,014	(5,553)	(358)
Opening bank balance	32	665	1,280	1,231	6,245	1,050
Closing bank balance	33	£1,280	£1,231	£6,245	£692	£692

provision for them on the VAT returns. The totals are accurate in spite of not being precise because the rounding tends to cancel out to within a pound or two. Precise figures are an unnecessary nuisance in a report like this because pence take up more space and make it harder to read.

The first line is the value of debtors (accounts receivable) at the beginning of the week. It is the same as the closing debtors from the previous week. If this is the first time you have produced the report, you will have to add up all your outstanding sales invoices to get the total.

If you have a sales ledger, the total of the account balances is the figure you need. If your ledger is being correctly maintained you will have a sales ledger control account, which will give you the total. In that case I suggest that you check that it agrees with the sum arrived at by listing all the account balances just in case there is an error. It is as well to start with the correct figure.

Next come several lines for the sales invoices issued during the week. I analyse my sales under separate headings for the key parts of my business. Even small businesses can benefit from breaking down their sales into the main categories. Yours might be by department or by location rather than by type of sale. If you have a number of them, it might be better to show the detail on a sub-schedule. I have only a few so I put them all on the main one.

I separate my fee income from expenses recharged to my clients, such as travel, motor and telephone, because these non-profit items otherwise inflate the figures and give a false impression of the real sales. Also I need this analysis for my annual accounts. I like to deduct the recharges from the respective expense headings to show the net cost to me. Doing the analysis this way means more information during the year and less work at the end of it.

The subtotal for standard rated sales, line 5, makes it easy to see my true income total. There's one other income line – for books – which is separate for the reasons explained below.

The subtotal for standard rated outputs, line 9, gives me the figure on which the VAT shown later on line 12 should be 15 per cent – VAT has to be added to expenses recharged as well as to fees. This is a very useful quick check, which proves that both the individual calculations on my invoices and this summary of the figures taken from them are correct. That is valuable because errors in charging VAT can be expensive if the VAT man finds them later when it is too late to collect from the customer. Errors in summarising tax for the return also mean an unexpected bill for extra VAT, if the mistake is against Customs. If it's against you, you have paid too much, which is bad and it might never be found. Often it is possible to protect against errors by laying out one's figures in such a way as to build checks into them and that is what I have done here. It suits my system to check the VAT on the cash flow report but, if you have a separate sales summary, it should be done there.

Books zero rated, line 10, is another income line so, to find my total sales, I must add it to the subtotal for standard rated sales. I cannot avoid the subtotal first because this line has to be where it is in order to permit the VAT check.

The total outputs and the VAT lines, numbers 11 and 12, give me figures which I need for my quarterly VAT return. The VAT is a substantial sum and line 12 enables me to keep an eye on the size of the amount I will have to pay. This will be reduced by the input tax I can recover but, in my kind of business, that is fairly small so the output total is a good guide.

The total invoiced, line 13, is the sum of all the invoices I have issued during the week.

When my book-keeper fills in the report, she skips line 14, the closing debtors, for the moment and enters the total of the cash received from debtors during the week on line 15. She then calculates line 14, the debtors outstanding at the end of the week, by deducting line 15 from the total of line 1, starting debtors, plus line 13, total invoiced.

The closing debtor figure is an important one in any business – yet many cannot quickly find out how much money they have tied up in it. This report gives me every Monday morning a running total adjusted for invoices issued and cash received. There can of course be arithmetical mistakes so we check the total every four or five weeks by adding up all the unpaid invoices. If the total of the unpaid invoices does not agree with the calculated figure we have to look for the error but, with practice, accuracy is not difficult.

If you have a sales ledger, your debtor total each week will come from your sales ledger control account as will the sales invoice and cash received totals. However, like many small businesses, I do not keep a sales ledger. I simply have a file of unpaid invoices, which I have to add up in order to check the calculated total.

If you give cash discounts or issue credit notes to customers, you will need to adjust for these, as shown on the more sophisticated version of the report on page 108.

By comparing the closing debtors with the sales totals including VAT for the previous few weeks, I can keep an eye on how many weeks sales invoices are unpaid and thus how well my credit control system is working. I can also see what cash is likely to come in from my customers in the next week or two since I know the value of the invoices issued a month or so ago.

The next figures in the report are the main expenses which appear in the profit and loss account of my business. Since the number of headings is few, it is easy to show most of them. In a larger business one would lump the smaller ones together, as in the more elaborate example later. The figures come from the cheque book counterfoils or from the cash book, if you keep one.

In my case, 'petty cash', line 21, represents expenditure on postage and office sundries which are included in sundry expenses in my accounts. In a larger business petty cash might be divided over several account headings but it is convenient to have a line for these cheques. Which other expenses you should show separately depends on which are large enough to matter.

I show standing orders and bank charges at line 23 even though they are small because we do have to remember to pick them up from the bank statement when it comes. Otherwise an error will creep in which will be a nuisance.

The subtotal for expenses at line 24 is a guide to how the total costs are building up. The figures are not the same as the ones which will appear in the profit and loss account because they take no account of opening and closing creditors (accounts payable) or of the adjustments made in the annual accounts for such items as insurance or rates paid in advance. However, these are not very large and, usually being similar to the previous year, they tend to cancel each other out so that the payment totals are a reasonable guide. Of course, that will be less true for you if the total of you unpaid expenses varies a lot.

Next come payments which do not affect the profit and loss account. VAT, capital expenditure and drawings by the owners tend to be large sums relative to the finances of any business. In a limited company, it is important to keep an eye on drawings especially because, if and when the total exceeds any loan account, the cash must be subject to PAYE as salary. One cannot just remove cash when one wants to. It is either a repayment of a loan or it must be taxed. Like most owners of businesses, I pay various private items through my company, often because they are on the same invoice as a business expense. These private amounts are then charged to me as drawings. Showing the figures on line 27 helps me to keep an eye on the total.

In this example, the directors' salaries are included in the wages figure. You may prefer to show them separately from staff pay.

The deposit account, line 29, shows transfers to and from deposit. Thus, in the third week of the example, £2,000 has gone out on deposit. It was transferred in the week after the large influx of cash in order to allow time for the cheques to be cleared. If money is transferred back from the deposit account, it is shown in brackets on line 29.

Line 30 shows the total of all the cheques written each week.

Then we calculate the net cash flow for the week, line 31, by deducting the total paid out, line 30, from the money in, line 15. If the result is a minus, it is in brackets. Brackets show minuses better than red, if you will be photocopying the report. Adding or subtracting the net cash flow to and from the opening cash balance on line 32 – the same as last week's closing balance – gives me the new bank balance. Overdrafts are also shown in brackets.

Line 33 shows the bank balance as per my books. The bank's records probably show a higher figure on that day owing to some cheques not yet having been presented. On the other hand, some of the cheques from customers paid in during the week may not have been collected by the bank so the cleared balance, which is the one on which the bank works when calculating its charges, could be lower. Nevertheless the balance is the same as the one which would appear in a balance sheet drawn up at that date and it is a good working guide.

Two more points: first, the figures build up to totals every four or five weeks, not each calendar month. I do not believe in working in calendar months because of the inconvenience of an end in the middle of the working week. It is much easier in most businesses to run the totals to a weekend. Staff get used to working in accounting weeks more easily and jobs like counting stock or listing unpaid invoices tend to be done more efficiently at the end of a week, especially in a workshop or factory when there is pressure to get the work out. I therefore recommend that you divide the year into four 13-week quarters each of which subdivides into two four- and one five-week periods.

The cumulative totals give me an indication of my profit for the year to date. Whether it will do so in your business depends on how many other complications you have. The report is a better guide to profit in a service business than in one which has money tied up in stocks of goods for sale or work in progress. If you are are not sure why changes in stock levels do not affect cash in the same way as profit, see Chapter 11.

Depreciation and bad debts are not shown so one has to allow for these when using the report as a guide to profit.

The second point is that the figures reveal patterns after one or two periods. For instance, salaries and PAYE/NI payments appear at intervals. It could be important to show the total paid out to employees separately from the PAYE/NI. I do not bother but for many businesses the monthly PAYE/NI cheque is significant. A separate line highlights whether or not it has been sent.

Other bills like VAT, electricity and telephone appear quarterly. This helps to assess the position at a glance not only as of today but over the next month or two. The pattern of payments shows what major bills, such as VAT, are due shortly.

The report thus helps to avoid those unpleasant surprises which result if you overlook such a payment when relying on your bank statement. Not only does the report help one to control the cash properly, it saves much waste of time in checking up on whether key bills have been paid.

A cash flow report suitable for those who sell goods

The cash flow report I use in my business will suit many other small ones. The next example is more appropriate for a business which sells goods. It may suit you better or you could use part of both reports adapted for your needs.

This version is intended to be completed weekly like the one already discussed. However, only the totals for the period of four weeks are shown in the example, in order to fit the year to date figures for actual and budget on the page of this book. This shows how the report can be compared with your budget, if you have one. Incidentally, I see no point in comparing the period

Monthly cash flow report
4 weeks ended 30 September

Figures in brackets are minuses or overdrafts

	Line	Period actual £	Year to date Actual £	Year to date Budget £
Opening debtors	1	1,800	1,000	1,000
Add: Sales on credit inc VAT	2	1,600	4,700	3,600
Less: Closing debtors	3	(1,900)	(1,900)	(1,000)
Discounts allowed	4	(—)	(—)	(—)
Cash received from debtors	5	1,500	3,800	3,600
Cash sales inc VAT	6	3,600	11,500	11,000
Total cash from sales	7	5,100	15,300	14,600
Other receipts: Assets sold	8	—	200	200
Other	9	—	1,000	1,000
Total cash in	10	5,100	16,500	15,800
Opening creditors	11	2,050	1,300	1,300
Add: Bought ledger invoices inc VAT	12	3,500	12,250	10,600
Less: Closing creditors	13	(1,150)	(1,150)	(1,300)
Payments made – Bought ledger	14	4,400	12,400	10,600
– Cash items	15	1,380	3,560	4,200
Total cash out	16	5,780	15,960	14,800
Net cash flow	17	(680)	540	1,000
Opening bank balance	18	(1,780)	(3,000)	(3,000)
Closing bank balance	19	£(2,460)	£(2,460)	£(2,000)

Analysis of total cash out				
Net wages		90	280	420
NI and PAYE		—	—	—
Rent		—	260	260
Electricity		60	60	60
Telephone		—	20	20
Loan interest		—	50	50
VAT		270	270	270
Rates		—	290	290
Bank charges and interest		—	—	—
Insurance		—	100	100
Capital expenditure		—	500	1,000
Drawings		250	800	800
Income/Corporation tax		600	600	600
Petty cash		30	150	—
All other (inc goods and expenses)		4,480	12,580	10,930
Total cash out		£5,780	£15,960	£14,800

totals with the budget for that period. Differences in the timing of payments are inevitable. It is the totals for the year to date which matter.

The report begins as before with opening debtors and invoices issued. At line 4, it shows the deductions from sales needed if you allow cash discounts to customers. You might also want a line for credit notes issued to customers if you take goods back or if you have to adjust your customer's accounts for short deliveries, breakages etc.

There is a separate line, number 6, for cash sales because some businesses have a retail counter or sell for spot cash to some customers or to staff, as well as making sales on credit.

Lines 8 and 9 for other receipts can be important when assets are regularly sold, loans are received, or there are other exceptional receipts, which must not be confused with ordinary income. For instance, you would use the 'other' line, number 9, for money which you put into the business yourself.

Now we come to a new part of the report, at line 11, which is not in the more simple version. In many businesses, the total owed to creditors is an important figure. If you buy goods for resale, you are sure to need the information provided by this part of the report.

You get the figures in much the same way as those for debtors and sales. The opening creditors total is the closing one from last week or, when starting to use the form, the total of the balances on your purchase ledger, if you have one, or of your unpaid invoices from suppliers if you do not.

The invoices total comes from the purchase ledger control account or the purchase invoice day book if you have such records. If you do not, you will need to add up all the purchase invoices you received on credit during the week. Ignore for now any invoices which you paid immediately (see line 15) – just list those for goods or services which you bought on credit.

Then you jump to line 14, just as you did in dealing with debtors and sales above. You enter the total of the cheques written in the week to pay invoices received on credit. Then you calculate the closing creditors the same way as you did the closing debtors.

Most businesses pay a few bills immediately on receipt and these are not therefore entered in the purchase ledger. Line 15 is for the total of these cheques.

If you do not have a purchases ledger, you might find it

easier not to have to separate the 'immediate' payments from those for purchases on credit. You can avoid having to do so by including *all* invoices received in the figure on line 12. Line 15 is then unnecesary, all payments being shown on line 14.

The same remarks concerning accuracy apply as for the closing debtors figure in my comments on the simpler version of the report. It does not matter if there are minor errors or omissions. The key point is to have before you every Monday morning the approximate totals of what you owe and are owed.

The *pattern* of purchase invoice totals can be especially useful if the business has a heavy programme of either capital investment or seasonal stock building. However carefully you try to estimate the timing, a cash flow forecast made a year ahead can only be a guess. The cash flow report shows how the invoices are actually coming in, thus providing accurate information a month or so before the cash to pay them has to be found.

The remaining lines for net cash flow and the bank balance are completed in the same way as for the simpler version.

This version of the report omits the detail of the payments, which is shown on the simpler one. The reason is that to analyse the payments on the same sheet of paper would crowd the layout and make it more difficult to read.

I believe it is preferable to show the totals as per the example and to have a second sheet giving the payments in whatever detail is appropriate to your business. You do not need to show all the expense headings. I suggest you show the significant sums which are either easy to pick out, like the weekly or monthly salaries cheque, or are irregular, like capital expenditure, or are paid at intervals, like insurance. My suggested payments analysis is on page 108.

You may wish to adapt these examples anyway to produce your own version of the report to suit your circumstances. For instance, you might want to show output and input VAT separately from sales and purchase invoices on the second example to see how the net balance is building up.

Any business can have a weekly cash flow report. The figures needed are readily available whatever the state of your records. The effort required to produce it is minimal, yet it imposes a useful discipline in ensuring that key figures are added up each week. The report offers the following valuable information about the business:

- Your sales to date.
- How much your customers owe you – assuming you sell on credit.
- How much you owe your suppliers – if significant enough to be included in the report.
- How much cash you are likely to receive from customers and/or will have to pay out to suppliers over the next month – from the pattern of sales and purchase invoice totals.
- The totals of your costs paid out to date – which in many businesses will be a fair indication of how they are building up.
- If you do not hold significant stocks or work in progress, the report will often be a reasonable guide to your profit to date – before depreciation on fixed assets or bad debts, of course.
- Your bank balance – after taking into account all cheques written and all money banked up to date.

Action to be taken

This chapter has shown two versions of the cash flow report, one of the most valuable business tools in managing a business. Whether your business is simple or complicated, one of the examples can be adapted to suit it. However chaotic your records, all the information you need is available for a minimum of effort. In my business, all my staff have to do is to add up the figures on the sales invoices for the week's sales and to note the money in from the paying-in book and the payments from the cheque book counterfoils. The rest is a few minutes' arithmetic. What could be simpler!

So, no questions on this chapter – action! How about getting out your records now and drawing up your own report? Once you've got the routine going, someone can do the figures for you each Monday morning. The improved knowledge of your finances and the peace of mind which comes from having things under control will repay a hundredfold the effort to get it going. I know. I'm a qualified accountant; yet I muddled along without the report for ages before I made myself do it. Now I wouldn't be without it.

Chapter 14

How to Get Your Customers to Pay up More Quickly

Why it matters

If you sell on credit, there's always too much money tied up in debtors (accounts receivable). The tank chart in Chapter 11 showed you how cash is absorbed this way. To defeat the tendency for debtors to use too much of your money will require your best efforts and most earnest attention. It will be worth it because, together with stocks of goods, this aspect of your business will soak up cash quicker than any other if you let it. Many others do let it. Letting customers borrow too much money by not enforcing payment on time is expensive and often restricts a business's ability to invest in its future.

For example, suppose your sales including value added tax for the last three months were as follows:

	£
Jan	30,000
Feb	40,000
March	30,000
	£100,000

Your invoices are due for payment 30 days after their date of issue so, theoretically, only the March ones should be unpaid on 1 April, value £30,000.

Suppose your customers in reality take on average two and a half months' credit; the figure will in fact be £85,000, ie March plus February plus half the January invoices. So your customers have £55,000 more of your money than they should.

Worse still, if your sales are standard-rated at 15 per cent, and your VAT quarter ends on 31 March, you will have to pay the government a month later on 30 April the VAT on the March and half the February sales which you will still not have collected. Since the figures include VAT, that means a further drain of $3/23 \times £50,000 = £6,522$.

A good credit control system has a vital part to play in ensuring that the money comes in when it should because, if you do not ask for your money on time and you do not make a fuss if you do not get it, customers will get the message that you do not mind.

Bad credit control costs a bomb!

1. You pay interest on a higher overdraft or fail to earn it on money on deposit.
2. Chase-up letters cost money plus time of staff who could be better employed on more productive tasks.
3. Your bad debts are higher because they are not spotted early. Not only do some become bad merely because you are last rather than first to be paid, but you probably go on supplying long after a good system would have warned you to stop throwing good money after bad.
4. Money in debtors, which ought to be in the bank, cannot be used to develop the business.

Let's have the right information

First, work out what the value of your debtors ought to be, using the sales figures for the last few months, not the annual average. Seasonal variations often make averages meaningless.

Add VAT, if applicable, to the sales figures since it is included in the sums owed to you.

Adjust also for credit balances on your sales ledger – amounts owed by you to customers rather than owed by them to you. Often the balances are artificial, being the result of accounting errors or special situations, and the total may be large enough to distort the statistics. Show the gross sums owed to you and any credit balances owed by you as separate totals. The true position will probably be shown by using the gross total for your statistics, not the net one.

If there are any large customers who pay on special terms, whether very quickly or more slowly than the rest, it may be necessary to eliminate both sales to them and the amounts outstanding from them from the totals of sales and debtors in order to see the true picture for the majority to whom your normal terms apply. Export customers are often an example of those to whom special extended credit terms apply, if only because of the delays in collecting money in foreign currencies around the world.

Having found out the true position as to how many days' sales are outstanding you can then measure the difference on what it ought to be and can assess how serious the problem is and therefore how much attention it merits.

In any case, you will not remedy a bad situation overnight. If your customers are used to taking two and a half months' credit, they will have to be retrained. This can be done by adopting a firm policy properly enforced but it will take time to cajole, persuade or threaten them into paying on time. How long will depend upon which industry you are in and your relationships generally with your customers but, inevitably, they won't like being asked to stop keeping your money longer than they should and some may take umbrage.

However, the risk of offending customers by requiring prompt payment is a short-term one. Once they know your policy and that you mean to enforce it, customers are usually willing to pay more or less on time. Generally speaking, not much worthwhile business is obtained by allowing long credit. The bad payers tend not to be worth having as customers.

The need for a policy on credit terms

Getting your debtors to pay up on time demands careful attention to detail. Have a policy on credit. Set time limits and make sure your customers and your staff understand them. Show the terms on price-lists, invoices and statements, and write welcoming letters to new customers quoting them.

Good credit control is largely a matter of habit on the part of both your customers and your staff. If your customers know that you expect them to pay promptly they are much more likely to do so than if you often let matters drag on. This is especially true in organisations big enough to employ clerks to process invoices. These staff soon get to know who presses them for payment and who does not and they tend to set their priorities accordingly. Well, you would too in their place! Don't be intimidated by large organisations, however. Their different departments usually do not talk to each other much. One can often make personal contact with the accounts staff who can ensure payment of invoices without in any way affecting the relationship with the buyer.

Are your credit terms clear?

Wording such as 'Net monthly' or 'Payment is due on the 21st of the month following' is vague and an invitation to your customers to interpret it in their favour. Be precise, with wording like 'Payment should be received by us within 30 days of the date of this invoice' or 'Payment of all invoices should be received by us not later than the 21st of the month following that in which they are dated'. Perhaps you can shorten the above while remaining specific but there is too much money at stake for brevity to be the main consideration.

Print the terms clearly on your invoices and statements, on your acknowledgements of orders too if you have them, so that they cannot be missed. Do not hide them apologetically in a corner as if they do not really matter!

Credit limits

If you sell regularly to the same people, set limits for credit to individual customers and see that your sales records show when a limit is being exceeded. This is especially important for new customers but it can also be a useful protection against something suddenly going wrong with a long-established one who pays regularly. If you use a computer, it may be able to calculate automatically a limit based upon average orders for each account for, say, the last six months. A balance exceeding the limit then triggers a signal prompting a check on the circumstances.

Control in the order office

Put your policy in writing to the staff in the order office who must prevent goods going out to overdue accounts. Organise a system for producing up-to-date details of those who are over their credit limits or who are on the 'stop' list for non-payment, *and enforce it*! Do not go on handing out goods or services to customers whose silence already indicates that they may not be going to pay.

In every industry there is a hard core of undesirable customers who run up bills with any supplier who allows them to do so. Then, when the supplier finally stops deliveries, they move on to some other source of easy credit. Once gone, they never come back.

By being tough, you minimise such losses and you may even retain some of this floating business.

Opening new accounts

The sales staff must understand the credit terms, upon what basis they can open new credit accounts, and whose authority is required.

The moment a new customer asks for credit is the time when he can be asked for references etc. The minimum information which should be asked for is as follows:

Is he a sole trader, partnership or limited company?
Who are the owners/partners/directors?
How long in business?
Full address and telephone number.
If a new business, what is previous career of the principals?
What is the nature of the business?
If a limited company, is a guarantee of the directors available?
Or up-to-date accounts?
If a new business, how is it being financed?
What trade references are available?
What credit limit is needed to cover the expected business?

Vary this list of questions to suit your trade. It may seem formidable but in practice potential customers often appreciate the efficiency of the supplier who does take the trouble to check them out. It is particularly important to know the background of a limited company. They tend to have a spurious credibility because of the 'limited'. In practice, since the liability to creditors is indeed limited, doing business with them is often riskier than with a sole trader or a partnership.

Trade references can be valuable, particularly if they are from people in the same business as yourself. Do not be afraid to approach a competitor for an 'off the record' chat about a potential new customer. Often there is cooperation on credit because everyone has the same problem.

Beware of references given by the prospective customer. Many bad payers keep a few accounts up to date especially for use as references.

There are various trade protection societies and credit reference organisations who will supply information about customers, such as credit ratings, latest accounts filed if a limited company and so on. Try Yellow Pages or your Chamber of Commerce for local addresses. The London based national organisations advertise in such media as the *Financial Times*.

The Registrar of Companies, Companies House, Crown Way, Maindy, Cardiff CF4 3UZ; telephone 0222 388588, will supply a copy of the latest filed accounts of a company for a fee.

Get your bills out quickly

Get your invoices out as soon as possible after you have delivered the goods or done the work. It looks efficient and customers like confirmation of the price. Moreover until he has your invoice, the customer cannot approve it and put it into his payment system.

Can you make it easy for him to pay by including a payment slip, possibly a Giro one? Ask your bank for details of the Giro system.

Then get the statement out promptly and follow up as soon as the credit period is exceeded. Keep following up! Monthly intervals are much too long. My father used to say, 'Send them a postcard daily!' He exaggerated, but not by that much. Debtors soon notice at what intervals you chase them. Depending on your credit terms, a monthly statement should be followed by a polite overdue reminder a few days or at most two weeks later. Subsequent letters should be at weekly or fortnightly intervals – not three, four or more weeks later. The psychological effect of rapid follow-up is to convince the debtor that you really mean business, that you care about getting your money.

On the other hand, slow follow-up creates the opposite impression: that you do not mind that much, that it does not matter.

A debtor's willingness to pay is at its maximum in the initial credit period. It then declines rapidly as the bill becomes more and more overdue. Before long the debtor begins to feel he or she does not really owe the money and to resent attempts to collect it. This is psychological. I expect you've been a debtor in that situation. I have. So ask for your money promptly and keep on asking. Asking first often means being paid first.

All this, of course, requires an efficient accounting system capable of producing the necessary figures and details on time so that you can ask for your money.

How we do it in my business

An efficient system is not necessarily an elaborate one. In my business, we do not have a sales ledger with account cards for each customer. A ledger is really only needed if you have a lot of transactions with each customer, possibly involving credit notes for returns etc. Then the detail becomes hard to follow unless the transactions are all grouped together in a ledger account.

I simply have my secretary type three copies of each invoice. The customer gets the top copy; the second goes in numerical order on the sales invoice file; the third goes on the unpaid invoices file. When the invoice is paid, we write the date the cheque is received on the third copy which is then transferred to a paid invoices file. To see which invoices are outstanding, I therefore have to look through one file only, the oldest invoices being at the back.

We follow up first with a 'Have you forgotten?' sticker on a photocopy of the invoice 30 days after its date. Two weeks after this gentle reminder we send a brief letter signed by my book-keeper or my secretary. It gives them a little status and encourages them to operate the system. Chasing up is not delayed if I am away.

If after another two weeks, ie two months after the date of the invoice, it is still unpaid, we start getting upset. My staff telephone rather than write. So far I have not been involved, which means that I can now intervene if necessary either by telephone or in writing with a plaintive, 'My staff tell me my bill is unpaid. Is there a problem?'

Chasing the bad payers

If all this fails to get results, I do not mess about. I either put the matter into the hands of a collection agency or, if the debtor is a limited company, I threaten to apply to the court to have it wound up using wording similar to the following:

We write in respect of the outstanding amount of £XX for (state nature of goods or services you supplied) pursuant to our invoice date . . .. Despite repeated requests for payment including a letter on . . . and a telephone call on . . ., you have neglected to pay the amount due.

Accordingly we give you notice that if the amount of £XX is

not paid to us within three weeks from receipt by you of this letter we are to commence proceedings to wind up the Company on the basis of Section 123 (I)a of the Insolvency Act, 1986.

Yours faithfully

If that does not produce a response, the threat can only be carried out once various formalities have been complied with and there are costs involved in doing so. You cannot use s. 123 for a debt under £750 and it may not be suitable for use in a dispute in which your customer denies he owes you money, so you should take legal advice if you think you may have to take the required action. However, the threat itself is often enough to obtain payment or to extract the facts when a customer has been stalling because he is in financial difficulties.

This is not a textbook on credit control and the law so, for information on how to sue your debtors in the courts, go to your lawyer, a specialist book or one of the debt collection agencies.

Everyone has some slow payers. I maintain that the longer they are left, the slower they will pay, if they pay at all. So I repeat, asking first often means being paid first: pressing for payment quicker than other suppliers will at least prevent you throwing good money after bad and it may mean that you are the one who gets paid. Discover the bad news as soon as you can. You may even be able to help your customer by making a sensible arrangement under which he pays off the debt while you continue to supply against cash on delivery.

Train your staff

Credit control is often a junior function with low grade staff. Train them. Do not let sales and marketing dominate with all attention on getting and filling orders and none on obtaining payment. Your staff need to know you care about credit control before you can expect them to operate a tight system. Yet once they are properly trained and motivated, they can do most of the work for you.

If your clerks are to chase customers for payment without giving offence, they must be taught how. Good liaison with other departments is essential so they know if there are any reasons for delayed payment such as disputed or incomplete deliveries, quality problems etc. A pleasant telephone manner and an ability to write good letters are important. The way your people ask for payment can improve or undermine your image, just as much as the salesman who visits.

In particular, complaints which your follow-up system unearths should be documented and dealt with efficiently. Do you have an analysis of complaints on which to base effective query control and remedial action? Are your people trained to press for the balance of the money not in question, leaving just the disputed amount unpaid?

Cash discounts

Giving cash discounts is a poor substitute for good credit control.

The true cost of a discount of 2½ per cent for payment at 30 days is the price reduction related to the number of days by which payment is received earlier. So, if customers would normally pay at 65 days on average, the calculation is:

$$\frac{2.5}{97.5} \times \frac{365}{35} = 26.7\%$$

This is an expensive way to obtain prompt payment. And do your customers really take 65 days? Suppose it is 45 days on average and you allow three days of grace for the discount, you only receive your money 12 days earlier. Then the real cost of the discount is:

$$\frac{2.6}{97.5} \times \frac{365}{12} = 78\%$$

Similar calculations apply to 3.75 per cent at 7 days for which, usually, the true period in practice is 10 days. If your customers would pay net on average at 45 days anyway, your interest cost is:

$$\frac{3.75}{96.25} \times \frac{365}{35} = 40.6\%$$

Many companies have found that an efficient invoicing, credit control and cash collection system can reduce debtors and cut credit periods without any need to offer cash discounts. If you offer them, ask yourself whether you have to for some reason or whether you could cut them out. That you may have always offered a discount and that most others in your trade do so are not sound reasons for continuing the practice, given the high cost.

Interest on overdue accounts

To threaten to charge interest on an overdue account is not usually an effective means of obtaining prompt payment in practice. The rate charged must of course be high or customers may simply use you as a lender!

If your claim for interest is to be enforceable in law, the terms must be clearly notified to your customer in advance. This means, at the very least, showing them on your order acceptance stationery or in correspondence regarding the order as well as on invoices and statements.

Dealing with major companies

Do not hesitate to apply your normal procedures simply because the customer is a household name. Remember Rolls-Royce went down! It may not be appropriate to ask for trade references or annual accounts but you should certainly find out who will be responsible for approving your bill and where the purchase ledger is located. Make contact with the customer's chief accountant or whoever is in charge of payment accounts and politely make the point about your terms of business at the start.

Some major companies take extra credit from small companies as a matter of policy. Check with other small traders in your area about their experience. Submit your bills promptly – a big organisation genuinely needs more time to approve and process them for payment – and as soon as delays occur, make a fuss.

Major orders can bankrupt you

A prospective customer, a big company, perhaps a household name, enquires for a substantial quantity of goods. The potential business is tremendous – perhaps a quarter or more of your existing turnover – but of course they do have their own specifications which you must meet.

You are excited. You 'leap about', invest time in technical development and produce some samples. The reaction of the customer is enthusiastic. You investigate the production problems, spend hours with the customer's technical staff, more time and probably money in perfecting the technical process.

It looks great. The order is practically in the bag. It just has to go up to the Buying Committee at the customer's headquarters, but his technical staff and his buyer assure you that there will be no problem. Meanwhile, how soon can you start production?

Now you really get going. You order in materials, take your staff off other tasks to plan the operation. You buy new equipment and mention a luxury cruise to your wife. Everything's running smoothly – your organisation has turned itself upside down to meet the challenge but you're ready to start next month – as soon as you get the order.

You never do get the order. At the customer's HQ the proposals are turned down – a change of policy, new buyer, technical problems – the reasons hardly matter, you're not going to get the order.

And you've spent money on research and development, materials in quantities you cannot use, equipment now not needed – without any commitment by the customer! Tough!

It happens to others regularly; do not get caught by this kind of 'bad debt'. As soon as material sums of money and/or time are involved, ask for money. It might be a contribution to costs or a commitment to pay them or a firm order. What matters is a legal obligation at least to see you do not lose money. Get it in writing – the executive you are dealing with may not have authority to place orders and asking for a written commitment will force any problem into the open. Don't place firm orders for materials or equipment until you have one yourself.

One businessman I know takes his accountant along once negotiations start on the financial aspects of a deal. The accountant looks severe and says 'no' at critical moments. Not a bad discipline as well as a good negotiating ploy!

Tell the salesman what's happening

The salesman's function is to sell but he should do so intelligently. Make sure that he understands the reasons for having credit terms and that he is able to justify them to customers. It is better to avoid using him to collect money unless this is normal trade practice, because it may be more difficult for him to get appointments if the customer knows that a cheque will be asked for. Moreover, if the system depends upon your salesman calling, any delay or missed dates owing to sickness, holidays etc slows up the money coming in. If the salesman only calls, say, every six weeks that is serious because his failure to do so provides the perfect excuse for your customer not to write that cheque.

Do see, however, that your salesmen are aware of your slow payers. It is hard for them if they call unawares on an account just after the customer has had a confrontation with your accounts staff.

The salesman's authority to vary credit terms must be clear

It is up to you to decide, in the circumstances of your business, whether to let your salesman allow extra credit. In most businesses, it is better not to because of the clash of priorities this creates. The natural tendency of all salesmen is to sell however they can and to permit them to give extended credit is likely to be an expensive way of getting orders.

However, it can pay off to make exceptions for customers starting up or short of cash for some special reason. Here creative credit control can sometimes build a customer into a larger account with a long-term loyalty to you because of the way you helped him in the early days.

If salesmen are authorised to propose longer credit in such special cases, the deal should be subject to approval by the office. Put it in writing and explain that it is a temporary concession, state the payment dates agreed and limit the period and/ or value involved.

Do your salesmen update your account details?

How many of *your* suppliers irritate *you* by invoicing you with the name of your business incomplete or wrong, with silly errors in the address or even in the name of the previous owner or occupier of the premises? Often the problem starts because sales staff do not inform the office when a business changes hands or because orders are carelessly made out.

If your own invoices contain such errors, this is bound to aggravate your credit control problems, if not actually to cause bad debts. How can you sue a business if you do not have the correct name?

Can your order forms or other sales stationery include a box for confirming or correcting the invoicing details?

Bad debts are no good to anyone

Remember that a sale on credit is not complete until you are paid. Bad debts not only lose you the value of goods supplied plus the VAT charged but also cost money to administer. A sale which is not paid for is better not made.

Suppose that you work on a gross profit margin of 20 per cent. A bad debt of £115 will therefore have cost you £80-worth of goods plus VAT of £15 on the value of the sale. To recover that £95 you will have to make further sales of £475 or *five times the loss*.

Credit insurance

You can insure against bad debts. Trade Indemnity Company Ltd, 34 Great Eastern Street, London EC2A 3AX; tel. 071-739 4311, charges fees which are variable according to the amounts and periods of credit allowed to your major customers.

The Export Credits Guarantee Department, Export House, 50 Ludgate Hill, London EC4M 7AY; tel. 071-382 7000, provides cover for overseas. Apart from compensating you for most of your loss, ECGD can help with advice on the creditworthiness of foreign countries and customers.

Do you export?

Apart from the services of ECGD mentioned above, there are various aspects of financing foreign credit to be considered.

You will need to learn about letters of credit and bills of exchange, for instance. Ask your bank for advice. Ask them also about the various ways in which payment can be collected from overseas.

For instance, in whose currency will the letter of credit or bill be stated? In which country will it be payable and at what bank?

Some banks are much better at collecting money from overseas than others. The American banks have sometimes been the best. The United Kingdom clearing banks have often been appallingly slow. The position varies according to the country involved and it is changing as a result of increased competition so it may pay to ask round. Do not necessarily rely on your domestic bank.

These may seem minor technical points but they can have a considerable effect on how long cash is tied up in export deals.

Summary

Good credit control is good business management and your customers will appreciate it as much as you do. The best of them prefer to deal with efficient suppliers and do not resent being held to terms of business providing that those terms are fair, in accordance with normal trade practice, and are clearly understood by them.

Sometimes it is indeed possible to retain a customer and help him to build his business by refusing him credit. This may prevent him from overtrading and may make him run his affairs that much more efficiently so that he stays in business and remains your customer.

There is no quicker way of losing customers than to allow them to take extended credit and then have to chase them for it, whereupon they go to other suppliers. In the long run little worthwhile business is obtained by being too easy on credit.

Success in minimising the cash tied up in debtors demands a good system, carefully thought out and systematically applied.

Chapter 15

How to Control Your Money Tied up in Stocks

Many businesses have more money tied up in stocks of goods for resale or of materials than in other assets. If stock is one of the biggest figures in your balance sheet too, failure to control it could sink you.

Stock control is a big subject. Many businesses have elaborate systems based upon sophisticated techniques. Computers and other electronic equipment are making possible far more detailed control even for small companies. This is not a dissertation on these systems – just a collection of common-sense points and hints for the practical manager on what causes excess stock and how to avoid it, especially in the smaller business.

Clever systems are a great help in controlling stock but common sense and simple good management will always be more important. All the systems can do is provide information about the results of the way you manage your stock. They may help you take decisions but they cannot make them for you.

Why stock control matters

Stock eats up cash faster than any other aspect of a business. The tank chart on page 85 shows you how this happens. It is easier to buy goods than to sell them so there are always some items which sell slowly, if at all. Since the mistakes remain and the successes have to be replaced with more of the same, one's stock tends to get bigger and bigger. If uncontrolled this results in more and more money being tied up in lines which you cannot sell until, one day, you run out of money to restock with the ones you can.

As a general proposition, holding stock is bad news

People sometimes kid themselves that holding stock is a worthwhile 'investment'. Normally that cannot be true. It may be when inflation is in double figures or when there are shortages of goods or materials, but only for some items. Extra purchases of these may pay off either because of the extra profit from inflated selling prices, or increased business resulting from being able to hold prices while stocks last, or because the goods may be unobtainable later.

The problem is to know which items will pay off. However severe inflation is, there are always some goods which do not sell even if the original price is maintained. As for supposed shortages, buying ahead of your needs is speculating. If you want to gamble on commodity prices, fine, but do not kid yourself that it is a normal business operation.

The one exception to the general rule of buying only for your immediate needs is when your business relies on a key component which you expect to be in short supply and which is produced by only a few sources. Microchips are a possible example for a manufacturer who uses them in his products.

Of course you must have adequate stocks to supply your customers. The problem is how to minimise the cost of doing this, given that the money tied up not only earns no interest but tends to lose value.

There are too many causes of stock wastage for stockholding to be other than an expensive exercise in most cases.

How stock loses its value

The expense of holding stock has been estimated at 25 per cent of its cost each year, allowing for interest on the money tied up and wastage. Some causes of wastage are:

- *Damage* in handling – especially if stockrooms are overcrowded owing to large stocks.
- *Deterioration* during long storage – dusty packaging can make an item unsaleable for instance.
- *Evaporation* and other natural reductions in quantity or quality.
- *Obsolescence.* You no longer make the product of which it was part, your supplier has updated the product or there is a new product which does the same job better. Computer games are an example of rapid obsolescence as more elaborate ones are invented and the computers themselves are altered.

- *Changes in fashion*. Women's clothes are only one example. Fads come and go for things such as home snooker tables and skateboards: and who remembers the hula hoop?
- *Over-buying*. You buy too many because you overestimate sales, count your stock wrongly, overlook a parcel of stock or duplicate an order. As a result stock is held past its 'sell by' date or the end of the season or is in such quantity that it cannot be sold or used in production within a reasonable time.
- *Pilferage*. Customers, staff and delivery drivers will all take your goods without paying if you put temptation their way by not having good controls. Obviously the more stock you have, the easier it is for some to get 'lost' without it being noticed.

The problem of pilferage

Pilferage takes many forms from outright theft, such as shoplifting, to minor misuse by employees such as writing private letters on company stationery or using equipment, vehicles etc, for private purposes. Often staff regard such use as a perk of the job and it may be tolerated or even accepted as such by the employer.

The problem starts with you, the boss. If you do not show you care, you cannot expect employees to mind, even if they are honest, decent people.

Showing you care means devoting time to sensible controls both physical and on paper. Valuable stocks should be locked away and access restricted, all goods being booked out.

In a tobacconist's shop, for instance, the owner cannot record sales off the shelves but he can note the number of packs of 200 cigarettes taken from the stockroom to the shelves. Similarly a publican can record the issue of bottles of spirits to his bars.

Such records make it much harder for complete packs or whole bottles to disappear. In many businesses similar records can do much to reduce the risk of theft if only because they demonstrate that the management cares. The problem, of course, is to draw the line between paperwork which is worth doing and that which simply creates work. Part of the answer lies in concentrating upon the more valuable and more attractive items. By establishing some checks on your goods you can do much to reduce temptation and keep people honest. If, on the other hand, you presume upon their honesty, you will have trouble sooner or later.

Watch those delivery men
Those who deliver goods to you must be controlled just as carefully as your customers or your staff. Never allow them to off-load goods direct into your stockroom. Ideally you should have a separate reception area so that there is no possibility of incoming goods being mixed up with stocks or with despatches to customers. Goods arriving should either be checked at once or should be signed for as 'unexamined'.

Here are some of the ways in which many delivery drivers regularly steal. Do not let them do it to you!

- If the quantity off-loaded is not checked the driver retains a parcel on the vehicle or, in the case of, say, petrol or oil, the tank on the vehicle is either not emptied or is not full in the first place. If the quantity is checked, the driver off-loads the correct amount but picks up a parcel and puts it back on the vehicle when the checker's back is turned.
- If access to the parcels is possible, the driver extracts part of the contents prior to delivery.
- If the goods come in different qualities the driver delivers a lower grade than ordered, then sells the better grade elsewhere, possibly splitting the difference with another customer who ordered the lower grade.
- If the driver collects empty containers for credit, a smaller quantity is recorded than is uplifted. Or a crate of full ones is removed instead of empties.

Hidden costs of stockholding

Too much stock takes up valuable space, makes it difficult to bring in new lines, change policies to meet new conditions etc. It may even clutter your premises so much that you cannot find items when they are wanted.

Thus excess stock can generate many hidden costs, lose you opportunities owing to shortage of space or cash, and generally reduce the efficiency of your business. It simply does not pay to tie up more money in stock than you have to.

Basic rules of stockholding

1. Keep a tidy, well-ordered stockroom laid out to a system. A retailer should allocate space according to gross *profit* generated (*not* gross sales *value*).
2. Keep records of stock and orders placed so that you have facts upon which to base each order.
3. Do not leave the ordering of fresh supplies to junior staff. Orders prepared by them on the basis of past sales should be scrutinised by someone who can assess future demand and is aware of plans for new products etc which may affect the need to reorder. A routine order for materials involves spending a substantial sum. Yet in many businesses, a clerk can place such an order whereas a new desk costing a fraction of its value requires the authorisation of the boss.

   Since surplus materials may be difficult to sell or even valueless to anyone else and the desk can always be sold off quickly, the priorities are all wrong.

Why surplus stock gets bought in the first place

Some of the causes are:

- Failure to match purchasing and/or production to sales, ie continuing to buy in normal quantities when demand has started to drop or when a product is to be discontinued or suspended.
- The 'just in case' syndrome. 'We had better have a few just in case someone wants one.' This attitude is typical of factory staff or shop managers if they are criticised for failure to meet demand but receive no praise for keeping stocks low.
- Producing in long production runs in order to use machinery efficiently. Quantities of slow selling goods which take too long to clear.
- Buying in quantity to obtain cheaper prices. This is rarely worthwhile and can amount to commodity speculation. See the story about table lighters opposite.

Do your suppliers deliver when scheduled, not before?

Suppose you order 10,000 units of a container for your product to be delivered over the next five months at 2,000 per month. To minimise his production cost, your supplier may produce all 10,000 in a single run. You do not want them all now partly because you do not have enough space for them and partly because you have agreed to pay on delivery.

At your supplier's factory, however, they too are short of space. Maybe their foreman decides to put 5,000 on a lorry for delivery to you, not 2,000. If your goods reception system is not adequate to identify the over-delivery of 3,000 and your staff do not realise what is happening, they will probably allow the driver to off-load the surplus. The result is not only an over-crowded stockroom but also an invoice for 5,000 units due now, not 2,000. Even if you spot the try-on at this stage, you are in a weak position, having taken delivery.

How I got caught on the lighters – or the bargain that wasn't!

Once long ago when I was young and green, I owned a small shop which sold cigarettes and gifts. The Ronson salesman called with a really special offer. If we bought their full range of 12 lighters, Ronson would throw in a thirteenth. Free!

The arithmetic went something like this:

		£
12 lighters: normal cost, say		78.00
Normal selling price (ignoring VAT), say,		120.00
Normal profit margin	35 %	42.00
Add selling price of thirteenth free lighter		12.00
Special offer profit margin	45 %	£54.00

45 per cent profit sounded good to me. My manager wondered whether he would sell the more expensive lighters, whose retail price ranged from £3 to £25, but he was persuaded by me to take the offer.

We sold two lighters fairly quickly – two of the cheaper ones – and four more over the next nine months. Three years later, we still had three left – not the most expensive but with a retail value of £45. We never did sell them! So instead of making £54 we made £9 and took three years to do it. It was a bad offer for us – we would have done much better to buy only the three or four lighters we could sell fairly readily and forget the rest.

This is a true story incidentally (though I have adjusted the prices) which happened in the late 1950s! Before Ronson sue me for libel, let me add that there was nothing wrong or unethical about their offer. The products were fine but we were the wrong shop to sell the full range.

Next time someone makes you a special offer if you will buy extra goods, remember:

- that you have not earned that lovely fat margin until you have sold the *last* one, not the first. The last one is always the hardest to shift.
- that special offers are really nothing special at all unless you know you can sell the extra quantity quickly. Otherwise, given the cost of holding stock, you will do better to buy only what you need now, especially if, as with those lighters, you have to take the full range, not just the quick sellers.
- that the manufacturer or wholesaler may be trying to shift slow-moving stock. If he has to offer a special deal, why do you suppose you will sell these lines when others are probably having difficulty in doing so?

There is nothing unethical in the supplier making you a special offer – but make sure it is special for you too, not just for him!

Some points on reducing your stocks

The amount of stock which a business must hold is partly decided by the time it takes to obtain more. Can you reduce the quantities you buy by obtaining more frequent deliveries from suppliers or by using local wholesalers rather than buying direct?

Using cash and carry wholesalers may not be appreciably more expensive when you take into account the costs of holding stock resulting from having to take the minimum orders and to accept the delivery cycles of manufacturers who supply you direct.

If you manufacture yourself, can you shorten your production cycle, thus cutting the stocks you need to hold because you can produce more readily to meet demand? Shortening the cycle often means that stock can be held as raw materials suitable for various products or possibly resaleable as it is, rather than as work in progress or finished goods which are probably useless for any other purpose.

Can you simplify your production in order to use common components for some products?

What is your policy if a customer wants just a few of an item for which your suppliers or considerations of production efficiency dictate larger quantities? Do you charge a premium to cover the surplus stock cost?

Set stock and reorder quantities

Do not leave the amount of stock held and the reorder quantities to the whims of your buyer or stock records clerks. Set figures item by item based upon a policy geared to your delivery times and your plans for new products, budgeted sales etc.

Do you deliver on time?

A British Institute of Management survey of 186 manufacturing plants showed that:

> 40 per cent did not formally monitor performance against promised delivery dates.
> 3 per cent had delivered *nothing* on time.
> 20 per cent had delivered 90 per cent of orders on time.
> 3 per cent had delivered everything on time.
> Overall, shop floor production efficiencies were no higher than 30 per cent.

Do you know what your figures are? Much of this appalling inefficiency results from failure to have the right items for each order in the right place when they are needed. A poor delivery record could indicate bad stock control: it certainly means you aren't shifting the stuff through efficiently so your whole system must be clogged up.

Why errors in valuing your stocks can wreck your figures

Since the stock figure is often so large in relation to others in the balance sheet, errors in pricing it can have a disproportionate effect on the net profit. For example, suppose the true value of your stocks is £100,000 and your correct net profit before tax is £50,000. A 10 per cent over-valuation of your stocks, £10,000, will overstate your net profit by 20 per cent.

The arithmetic gets worse still with a company which is in trouble. Because sales are too low, the quantities of stock are often too high owing to difficulties in achieving sales. Over-valuations are both more likely and less easy to spot because of the number of items and the large sums involved. Suppose there is a true loss of £10,000; that same 10 per cent error would eliminate it, so that the business appeared to break even!

The way stock is priced is therefore important. The principle is that it should be valued at the lower of cost or present market value. It's no good putting something in at £100, because that's what you paid for it, if it is obsolete and you can only sell it for £20. So the first point is to be careful when counting stock to note all items which are over-stocked in relation to sales, damaged or whose value is doubtful for some other reason. There's nothing so useless as goods which have been around in your storeroom for a while and which you can't sell in the foreseeable future. The chances are that, if anyone else wants them, they'll only pay a fraction of the normal price. All doubtful items should therefore be written down to realistic figures. More comments on stock values are given on page 137.

Do you make your stock figures tell a story?

Stock-taking is a nuisance but it has to be done. However good your records system is, there will always be differences between the records and what is actually in the stock room. Moreover, many businesses do not have a running record of all items held – you cannot in a small retail shop, for instance, because it is not possible to record each sale.

An annual physical count or, better still, a quarterly one is therefore usually essential. It requires organisation and effort and possibly closing the shop or stopping production. Yet many businesses fail to marshal the resulting information sensibly so as to extract the maximum value from it.

On page 138 there is an example of a stock sheet suitable for use in many cases. The sheets should be divided into sections by type of goods, such as raw materials, work in progress and finished goods. Each of these should be subdivided into such headings as type of product or, for production stock such as containers, into bottles, caps, jars, lids, labels etc.

Where the same items are repeated, it helps to have master sheets typed with full descriptions which are then photocopied for use at each stock-take. The master can readily be updated for additional lines without having to retype the lot, and the amount of writing during the stock count is much reduced: greater accuracy results from fuller and more legible descriptions.

Analyse your stock values by type of stock

When the stock is valued, the value should not be added cumulatively from sheet to sheet. Each should be totalled separately and the total entered on a summary sheet for each heading, such as bottles, caps etc.

That way one can compare not only the *total values* for such categories as raw materials or finished goods from one stock-take to the next but *each sheet*. As you will find you have much the same items on each sheet from one occasion to the next, it becomes easy to spot the variations in value and quantity.

No longer are you looking at just a total of, say, £100,000 but at a list broken down into categories and headings. Mistakes in counting or calculating and excessive quantities of stock tend to be highlighted by comparisons with previous counts. The stock figure is often one of the biggest in the balance sheet and is also one of those in which mistakes are most easily made. Organising the stock sheets to permit these comparisons from one count to the next is a great help in getting it right, besides providing a useful guide to where your money is tied up.

The cost figures you use to value your stocks are important

The goods you expect to be able to sell should be valued at cost but this does not necessarily mean the latest price you paid. Be careful not to build in artificial profits in your stock valuation by pricing goods you bought some time ago at the latest manufacturer's increased price. Since raising your stock valuation increases your current profit, you'll pay tax too soon, even if you do sell the goods next year.

Example of a stock sheet

Stock sheet for .... *Date* ....

Type of stock .... *Sheet no.* ....

1. Is the stock on this page valued at cost (net of VAT) or selling price (including (VAT)?
   If at selling price it must be reduced to cost by deducting the average profit margin.
   Check that this margin reduces the price to cost *net of VAT*.
2. Unit of stock means the measure of weight, volume etc. State this if the quantity is not in single units or if there are different sizes of the same item.
3. All calculations of value to be rounded to the nearest £.

Description of item	Unit of stock	Quantity in stock	Price each	Value of stock	Remarks
		Total at cost		£	

Retailers' stock valuations

Many retailers work from selling prices because it is difficult to keep purchase records for large numbers of stock items. Having valued stocks at selling prices, they then take off an average retail margin.

This must be done carefully or it will be inaccurate, also distorting the profit artificially. If you analyse the figures into different kinds of stock or by department, as suggested earlier, it makes it easier to get the figures right because you can use the profit margins applicable to each kind of goods. This is especially important if they vary widely as between, say, cigarettes at 9 per cent and hardware at 30 per cent.

If you use retail prices including VAT, you must use margins which reduce the stock valuation to cost *before* VAT. VAT is not a part of your stock values as you have already recovered it.

Manufacturers' stock valuations

The professional accounting bodies recommend that manufactured stocks and work in progress should be valued to include the overheads incurred in producing them. Be careful if you do this. It is easy to over-value stocks by including too much overhead.

Never increase the price of individual stock items; always add a percentage on to the total stock value for overheads because otherwise you will not know how much overhead is included in the stock valuation.

If stocks happen to be rather high at your year end and you price every item to include some overhead, it is all too easy to inflate your profit by building in too much overhead. This will not show up in the figures of individual overheads charged in the profit and loss account because they are not affected. It is not the expense totals which are reduced but the stock figure which is increased. The effect is to cut the cost of sales: adding the overhead element as a separate figure in the stock valuation enables you to see its significance and to compare it with your overhead totals.

If you're not sure what I mean by this, try adding £6,500, 10 per cent of the existing value, to the stock figure in the example in Chapter 4 and work out for yourself how the other figures alter. The profit would rise by over 40 per cent because of carrying forward about 9 per cent of the running expenses as the over-heads part of the stock valuation.

I use the figures in the XYZ shop example because they are in this book. However, only a manufacturer would normally include overheads in the stock valuation, not a retailer or a wholesaler. The idea is that the cost of manufactured goods includes not only the materials and wages needed to produce them but the overheads of the factory as well.

This is a complicated subject and the way the figures are done varies from case to case. However, if overheads are included in your stock valuation, don't let the accountants blind you with science! When they have done the detailed cal-culations, look yourself at the end result to see if the overhead figure included in the stock valuation makes sense to you. Other-wise you could be storing up trouble by adding in a theoretically sound value for overheads, which doesn't exist in reality.

The 80/20 rule

In any bunch of statistics 80 per cent of the value is likely to be accounted for by 20 per cent of the items. This is true for stocks. If you can identify and give special attention to the 20 per cent of the goods you hold which account for 80 per cent of the value, you will be well on the way to an efficient stock control system.

The converse is that it may not be worth controlling the low value items at all. Nuts, bolts and washers on a production line may be best dealt with on free issue as required since the value is low.

Why have stock records?

- To compare stocks held with sales or usage and place orders accordingly, thus minimising 'out of stocks' in quick selling lines.
- To identify slow sellers so that they can be eliminated.
- To help plan trading policies based on successful lines.
- To help prevent over-ordering or duplicate ordering.
- To help locate particular items.
- To provide records for accounting and insurance valu-ation purposes.
- In some cases to help price goods.

Here is an example of a record card which a retailer might keep. It groups products by manufacturer, rather than by type of item, in order to facilitate ordering.

This layout gives at a glance the history of a line. Stocks have to cover the period from date of order to arrival of goods so there always have to be some in hand. Stock last time, plus the last order, minus the present stock gives the sales since the last order. When each order arrives ring the quantities to show they have been received or amend if necessary to actual quantities received.

Example of stock record for retail quick selling lines

Manufacturer's name: CADBURY											
Date	2/1			15/2			2/4			17/5		
Product	Sales	Stock	Order	Sales	Stock	Order	Sales	Stock	Order	Sales	Stock	Order
Milk Choc	15	50	—	20	30	10	20	20	20	15	25	—
Plain Choc	20	15	15	20	10	30	30	10	35	30	15	25
Assortment	30	29	40	44	25	60	65	20	50	35	35	15

How to make up a stock record file for a retailer

This type of record can be kept on the large lever arch files obtainable from most stationers. Make up permanent records for each supplier on pieces of card 1½ inches longer than A4 paper. Write the supplier's name along the top long edge and list his products down the left-hand short edge. Punch holes along the top long edge and place on the file. These permanent records do not have to be rewritten.

For the stock and order record sheets, use the pads of A4 ruled paper stocked by stationers. Turn the sheets sideways so that the lines run vertically and punch along the top edge but off centre. If you fold so that the left-hand edge is about 4 lines in from the right-hand one, the crease gives the centre for your punch.

Your stock and order record sheets on A4 paper will then be overlapped by the card underneath showing the product names which thus do not have to be rewritten when the sheets are full. All you need do is enter the date on the A4 sheets and head up the columns Sales, Stock, Order as in the previous example. Each sheet will take five such sections comfortably on each side giving you a quick reference to ten orders which is enough for quick selling lines. Since the file is loose leaf, new sheets can be inserted as needed.

Stock records for slow selling lines and manufacturing stock

Most of your slow selling lines should be of high value (otherwise why sell them?) and may require technical descriptions and other detail.

Similarly a manufacturer's components or materials may be ordered in large quantities which are called off in batches from the supplier, so the records may need to show what is outstanding elsewhere as well as on your premises.

Such items probably require a separate card per item. Complete stock control systems with stationery and binders are made by companies such as Kalamazoo plc, Mill Lane, Northfield, Birmingham B31 2RW or Twinlock, now a part of Acco Europe Ltd, Nepicar House, London Road, Wrotham Heath, Sevenoaks, Kent TN15 7RS. Details can be readily obtained from these companies and are not therefore given here. Many computer systems are now available for small as well as large businesses.

If your business is very small you can get by with your own hand-made stock cards. Properly designed systems save so much time that it is worth having one as soon as you can afford to. See the next heading, however, regarding the difference between stock control and stock recording.

You can only use your stock records to tell you what you have on hand if you are able to update the sales or usage column for each movement. This is usually not practicable for retail fast-moving lines.

The point at which it is no longer safe to rely upon periodic stock-taking is a matter of judgement. To update stock records for every issue or sale can be a slow routine, expensive in time and difficult to keep accurate. Yet a manufacturer, for instance, may need to have such records if only because it is not practicable to check the shelves every time someone wants information on what is available.

The difference between stock recording and stock control

Stock *records* tell you what you have got. A stock *control* system controls what you have got by recording every stock movement as it happens. Under such a system you cannot put stock in or take it out without generating the necessary paperwork.

The objective of a *stock control* system is to minimise your investment in stock while ensuring that you always have what you need and giving you up-to-date figures for stocks held at any time. Orders for fresh supplies are initiated, or at least suggested, as part of the system.

The difficulty is that such control systems are hard to make work in practice because they demand high standards both in systems design and in discipline within the organisation. It is all too easy for the system's stock quantities to cease to correspond with the physical reality, whereupon chaos results.

The best stock *control* system is Joe walking round using his eyes – plus accurate forecasts of future sales or usage. *Stock records* are an adjunct to Joe's eyes. So involve your staff in stock control. Explain your objectives to them and give them responsibility for helping to keep stocks low.

When your business gets too big for Joe's eyes to keep track, you have to start using your stock records for stock control but keep your system as simple as you can.

Beware of the wild claims made by computer manufacturers that they have a wonderful stock *control* system for you. They may have a good *recording* system which may be worthwhile if you recognise its role as being limited to helping you to make better decisions, by providing more accurate and up-to-date information than can be obtained by hand. Even that is a bold claim in many cases. For instance, suppose your factory or warehouse is at a different location from the computer. Your information will usually be at least a day, possibly two, out of date. The reason is that your despatch details, from which your sales invoices are prepared, and the production figures both have to be entered in the computer before the files can be updated.

That may not matter, or it may mean that the so-called control features of the computer system – such as producing draft production or buying schedules – are useless.

Stock recording is relatively simple, though it does require disciplined paperwork if the figures are to mean much. If you have trouble getting it accurate manually, a computer is unlikely to help. It may make matters far worse because it requires every stock movement to be documented. Even in small organisations, there is often no one person who knows what all the sources of stock movements are so it is not a simple matter to specify the system needs, let alone see whether the computer system meets them.

Stock *control* is not simple. It usually requires a high degree of sophistication and the smaller business normally will do better to rely on managerial decisions based on a good *recording* system. Computer people who do not make this distinction, and who try to sell you a control system, merely betray their own ignorance of what really matters in management and how a business works. Do not let them blind you to reality in their enthusiasm to sell you a system. The consequences could be dire, and they may not be around to pick up the pieces – not that it would help much if they were.

As the capacity and speed of small computers increase, the problems are becoming easier to beat. It is now more practical for staff to use terminals to update records as stock comes in and to produce an invoice or chit for each item as it is sold or taken to the production line. Nevertheless, stock control will always be one of the most complex tasks in business because it requires the acounting records to correlate with physical movements in the shop or the factory and to do so fast enough to help manage those movements.

Summary

Stock eats up cash. Uncontrolled, it will absorb so much money that it will prejudice the financing of the business and possibly even prevent you investing in new activities.

Cash put into stock is not 'invested'. On the contrary, every £100 of stock can easily cost you £25 in interest charges and wastage. Apart from the financial cost, too much stock will physically inhibit the efficient running of your business.

Keeping stocks low requires:

- An understanding of how the business works. Factors such as production or delivery cycles, policy on stock outs and relating purchasing to sales or new product development activity are crucial to decisions on what quantities of stock are needed. The quality of those decisions influences how efficiently stock is matched with the needs of the business.
- Sensible systems for recording and counting stock to enable

management to know what is happening and to base ordering upon facts rather than guesses.

- The careful attention of all employees in implementing the details of the system. If you forget to train your staff, they will screw up your stock control and, with it, your production or sales.
- A tough attitude to bargain offers.
- Good physical and paperwork controls.

Pilferage in one form or another will cost you dearly if you do not take precautions. These include physical and paperwork controls. If you want other people to respect your property you must show that you care about it yourself.

Chapter 16

Pricing Your Time

Charging the right price for your time is crucial to your success. Underprice it and, at best, you will work long hours for small reward: at worst your business will fail.

Do you sell time?

Have you thought what it is you really sell? Is it your time or is it goods? Window cleaners and accountants price each job on the time it takes, so they obviously sell their time. However, some businesses, which supply goods, are really selling time, although this is not always obvious at first sight. If you supply and fit parts, for instance, you probably earn most of your profit from the labour charge, not on the goods supplied. The profit margin on the latter is nowhere near as important as that on the time.

Consider this bill from a vehicle repairer:

	£
Spare parts fitted	100
Labour charge	40
Total	£140

How much profit do you think the invoice might include? We can work it (see opposite) out if we make some assumptions based on typical margins of mark-ups. If you've forgotten the difference between a margin and a mark-up, see Chapter 17.

The labour charge contributes substantially more profit even though the charge for parts is two and a half times bigger. And, if the bill was divided equally between parts and labour, ie £70 each, the respective gross profits would be £14 and £46.67 with labour thus contributing 77 per cent of the £60.67 total.

So do not be misled by the value of the parts; the real profit is on the labour. Efficient control of time in the workshop is the

	Invoice value £	Profit margin on selling price %	Mark-up on cost %	Cost £	Gross profit £
Spare parts	100	20	25	80.00	20.00
Mechanic's time	40	66⅔	200	13.33	26.67
Totals	£140			£93.33	£46.67

key to profitability. The profit on materials supplied is useful but it is small in comparison.

The point applies to many kinds of business. Other examples of people who often supply expensive materials, but who earn most of their profit from the labour involved, are jobbing builders, house painters and anyone who mends things.

Time is also often important to those who make things with their hands. For instance, a producer of arts and crafts is likely to find that much of the cost of each object is the time it takes to make it.

Contrast that with a manufacturer who uses machinery to make his product. If sales rise, he can produce more to meet demand by running his machines for longer hours or possibly by working them faster. If you are a craftsman working with your hands you have no such flexibility in your supply of time.

If you employ people, as in a repair workshop, you can, of course, expand your sales by taking on more staff. However, people are expensive to recruit and employ and they usually have to be paid whether or not there is work for them. Since each new employee therefore adds substantially to costs, it is vital that the time of the existing ones is properly controlled and correctly priced. Some businesses use outworkers, who operate from home and are paid by the item produced but that is not often practicable.

Is the garage charging an extortionate rate per hour?

In the above example the garage is shown as trebling the cost of the mechanic's time to earn a profit margin of 200 per cent. That may sound extortionate to you but it is not. One reason is that the real cost is much higher than his basic pay per hour, because of all the time, such as holidays, sickness, tea breaks etc for which he is paid but which is not charged to customers. The rate per hour for the time on each job must allow for all these non-chargeable hours.

If you work alone without any employees, you have the same problem. You can never charge out all the time you have. Apart from your own holidays or sickness, there are always administrative jobs to do like the book-keeping, reading official bumf or trade magazines, correspondence or filing and organising your day.

If you sell time, you must charge a lot for it

A little further on I explain how to work out how much time you can hope to sell and what to charge for it. But first, here's an important point. Because you have only a limited amount of time, you must charge a lot for it. If your price is too cheap, you'll find yourself working flat out for an inadequate reward. Life is then a vicious circle. You don't make much money nine to five so you work longer hours to improve the score. This has three unpleasant consequences:

1. You have little leisure and you don't see your family as much as you should.
2. You have little time to think, so it is difficult for you to plan the business properly.
3. You still don't earn a really good profit.

All of which is no good to you and is unfair to both your family and your customers. It is unfair to the latter because, if you're harassed and overworked, you'll tend to give them less efficient service; worse, you won't have the time or money to develop your business properly so your customers will suffer in the long run too.

So it's vital to charge enough for your time to give you a decent profit without having to work long hours. Then you have spare capacity either to earn 'super profit' or to develop your business by doing the long-term things which take time to pay off or – most important – to spend some time with your family.

Pricing your own time

Of these three examples which follow, two assume that you are self-employed without staff and therefore selling just your own time. The third applies if you have staff.

Example 1 is a person working freelance from home, such as a labour-only builder or a designer. Example 2 is for someone working from an office, probably with a professional qualification of some kind but still selling only his or her time. Example 3 deals with pricing the time of employees, whose hours you charge out.

The examples start by calculating the *number* of hours you have available. Then they list your expenses in order to arrive at a cost per hour including a basic wage for you. This tells you how much to charge for an hour to earn the minimum you need to live on, assuming reasonable success in selling your services. I suggest you now glance through the first example (on pages 150–51) and then read the following explanatory notes.

How many hours have you available to sell?

Allow for reasonable holidays including bank holidays. These may interrupt the working week by more than one day particularly if you have to work on the premises of your clients. Many businesses shut for an extra day. Some sickness must also be budgeted for.

I suggest at least four weeks' holiday because so many ordinary employees now get this entitlement. If you want to earn a good living in self-employment it is not realistic to budget for shorter holidays whether or not you actually take four weeks in the early years. Indeed, I feel that to compensate for the extra risk and responsibility of being on one's own, five or six weeks' holiday is a reasonable allowance.

I take at least six weeks, usually more although I do some writing while away! If you decide to plan for more or less than four weeks, alter the number of weeks when doing the costing for your business.

What is a reasonable target to sell?

While a building labourer may be able to sell 100 per cent of his time during a boom, in more normal times neither he nor any other self-employed person can hope to achieve this. The percentage will vary according to the occupation and the work involved to obtain each new assignment. In the building trades a man may obtain regular work from one or two builders but he is vulnerable to anything going wrong because he has so few customers. Only you can decide given the circumstances of your business what is a sensible budget for the time you can hope to sell.

If you sell more of your time than the annual total upon which the cost estimate per hour is based you will, of course, make extra profit. Use a conservative estimate of the hours you will sell to allow a safety margin. Do not include overtime in the number of hours upon which you base your costings because you should not have to work long hours to achieve your target. While the number of hours you work may be higher so may your costs. Moreover, the target is the minimum that you need to sell in order to earn a living, not what you might like to achieve.

The costs of being in business

The costs quoted are only typical figures at the time of writing. You should make your own estimates and work out what kinds of expense you will incur. For instance, you might have machine rental or depreciation costs together with repairs and overhaul of equipment etc. I have put only a minimal figure for advertising. You could spend this much on entries in two or three Yellow Pages directories alone. Don't underestimate your costs. Build in safety margins to your figures because there are always unexpected items. Costs have a nasty habit of coming out higher than you thought.

Though the working wage is set at £300 a week, you may be quite happy with a lower figure or may require a higher one. The figure used is for you to decide although it is not realistic to use one which is below what you could earn in a job. In 1989 the national average wage for manual workers was about £215 and was as high as £250 in some industries. The 'independence' of working for yourself is often illusory. Most self-employed people are in reality at the beck and call of their customers. One lacks the security of the regular pay packet and the additional stress and responsibility should earn you a higher reward than an ordinary job.

The only exception to this might be a top earning executive

who chooses to drop out of a high pressure rat-race type job because he wants a more relaxed lifestyle. If that's you, think carefully, however. The lifestyle will be different all right but it is unlikely to be relaxed. Working for oneself is hard work and underpricing one's time is a mistake as I explain in Chapter 18.

The pension and life assurance contribution figures

A self-employed person can make payments for a personal pension policy which are deductible from his earnings for income tax purposes and also receives favourable tax treatment in the hands of the pension company. The policy can include life assurance cover if desired. These valuable tax concessions mean that a pension policy is a tax efficient way of saving for the self-employed, who are not entitled to the state supplementary pension, only the basic one. As much advantage as possible should be taken of this relief.

The maximum you can pay is a percentage of your 'net relevant earnings' which are not necessarily the same as net profit. The percentage starts at 17½ per cent up to age 35 and then rises in stages to 35 per cent at over 60. Profits over £60,000 do not earn relief.

The rules changed in 1989. If you have a policy issued before the change, the rules are different. Retirement annuity relief applies with different percentages.

Since pension provision is an important element of tax planning for the self-employed, I think it should be added to the minimum acceptable weekly profit to calculate the target earnings required. This makes the latter more comparable with the salary you could earn in a job which carries a pension scheme as a fringe benefit.

The figures in the examples are just assumed sums, below the maximum permitted. In Example 1 below, for instance, a person under 35 could pay 17.5 per cent of the £20,800 total profit, or £3,640.

Technical terms used in the examples

Depreciation is explained in Chapter 4.

Professional fees for a sole trader or a partnership would be mostly the accountant's charges for preparing the annual accounts and agreeing the tax liability with the Inland Revenue.

If the business is a limited company, the accountant must issue an 'audit certificate' which involves higher fees as explained in Chapter 2. Apart from accountants' fees, the heading also covers legal costs. In the first year these could be substantial if a business or a property from which to trade has to be bought, a lease negotiated or a partnership agreement prepared.

NI means National Insurance. A self-employed person pays NI contributions in two stages. Class 2 are paid either by stamping a card weekly or by authorising the Department of Social Security to make direct debits monthly on your bank account. Class 4 are paid at the same time as your income tax and are calculated on the taxable profit agreed with the tax inspector.

Example 1: A self-employed person without an office

This is an example for someone like a labour-only building subcontractor, such as a bricklayer, who works on the customer's premises or a person who works from home, perhaps a designer. The figures are hypothetical to show you the principles involved in calculating your own costs. You will not necessarily have the same kind of expenses and the prices will probably have changed anyway by the time you read this, so you will have to do your own calculations.

All the costs quoted assume that you are registered for VAT. The first example projects annual sales at below the registration limit. If those were your figures, you would only register voluntarily if you were selling to other registered businesses who could recover the VAT you charged to them. If selling to private customers, it would be better not to register. Non-recoverable VAT would only apply to certain of your costs, insurance, for instance, being exempt. To cover the lost VAT, you would not have to raise your prices by as much as the 15 per cent entailed by registration.

The first question is how much time have you got to sell?

	Weeks
Number of weeks in year	52
Less: Own holidays	4
National holidays/sickness (Xmas/New Year 3, Easter 2, May, Spring and Summer) total 8 days + sickness, say 6 days =	2
Possible working weeks (if no major illness)	46

What percentage of that time can you sell?

85 per cent? Approx 39   weeks × 40 hours = 1,560 hours
75 per cent? Approx 34½ weeks × 40 hours = 1,380 hours
70 per cent? Approx 32   weeks × 40 hours = 1,280 hours
65 per cent? Approx 30   weeks × 40 hours = 1,200 hours

Costs of being in business

	£	£
Motor: Insurance and road tax	400	
Repairs and service	600	
Petrol: 240 miles/wk at 30/gal = 8 gals at £1.80 (net of		
VAT) = £14,40/wk for 46 wks, say	650	
Depreciation: Say 25% of cost of car £8,000	2,000	
		3,650
Advertising		400
Telephone		400
Insurance – business policies		100
Professional fees		500
Stationery and postage		150
Sundries		300
Total expenses	A	5,500
Profit required net of pension contributions		
Working 'wage', min acceptable say, £300/week for 52 wks say		15,600
Pension/life assurance: (see explanation on page 151), say		3,600
Private medical insurance, say		560
NI Class 2: in 1990/91 £4.55/week for 52 wks, say	240	
Class 4: on profit from £5,450 up to £18,200 so		
£18,200 − £5,450 = £12,750 at 6.3%, say	800	1,040
Total earnings required (before income tax)	B	£20,800
Total sales required to cover costs and earnings	A + B	£26,300

Which means:

At 85 per cent in 39   weeks £674/week or, for 1,560 hours, £16.86/hr ⎫
At 75 per cent in 34½ weeks £762/week or, for 1,380 hours, £19.06/hr ⎬ plus
At 70 per cent in 32   weeks £822/week or, for 1,280 hours, £20.55/hr ⎬ VAT if
At 65 per cent in 30   weeks £877/week or, for 1,200 hours, £21.92/hr ⎭ applicable

Round your hourly rate upwards to, say, £19.10 or even £19.50, *not* down to £19.00. Costs are always higher than you think, so build in a safety margin rather than take a chance by trimming your rate.

Example 2: A person working from an office

This person has only his time to sell but uses an office and has a part-time secretary/book-keeper. The costs quoted are mostly rather low. If the secretary were full time, the general office expenses would probably be higher and would have to allow more for the secretary's salary. For instance, the depreciation figure I quote here implies, say, £2,000 furniture and fixtures at 10 per cent and £2,500 for equipment such as a typewriter, photocopier etc at 20 per cent. This may sound a lot but the total soon mounts up even if you buy second-hand. If you need a computer or word processor, those figures are too low and your stationery costs will also increase.

How much time can be sold?
See the previous example. There are still only 46 weeks in the year.

Costs of being in business		£
Part-time secretary (inc employer's share of NI), say		6,000
Motor: As Example 1 but works mostly in office so		
business mileage less; petrol less and total £3,650 reduces		
by £400 to		3,250
Rent		3,500
Rates		1,500
Telephone		1,200
Light and heat		800
Insurance		200
Repairs and maintenance		200
Stationery and postage		400
Professional fees		600
Sundries		650
Depreciation on fixtures, fittings and equipment		700
Total costs	A	£19,000

		£
Profit required net of pension contributions, say		26,200
Pension/life assurance (see earlier explanation), say		5,800
Private medical insurance, say		560
NIC: Class 2: in 1990/91 £4.55/week for 52 weeks, say	240	
Class 4: on profit from £5,450 up to £18,200	800	1,040
Total earnings required	B	£33,600
Total gross fees required	A + B	£52,600

Since the required gross fees are double those in Example 1, the weekly or hourly rates will be twice those calculated earlier.

Example 3: A repair workshop with ten employees

How many hours can you actually sell?
Suppose your men work a 40-hour five-day week. Each day will include start-up, cleaning and close down periods, tea breaks, waiting time, stores issue queues etc. The exact nature of these depends upon the business but you are bound to lose some of the day in time which cannot be charged to customers.

You may find that you can only expect 80 per cent of the day to be actually devoted to chargeable time, in which case, of your available hours 46 × 40 = 1,840, you can sell 80 per cent = 1,472 hours per man.

What is your direct cost per employee?
The figures given illustrate some typical items making up the direct cost of employing staff. You may well have different items in your business but the principles will be the same.

Number of available working weeks: 46 weeks as for previous examples

Assuming 40-hour 5-day week, each man is present for	1,840 hours
If he does chargeable work for 80 per cent of the time, you can sell	1,472 hours

What are your direct costs per employee?		£
Suppose the average basic weekly wage of your people is		250.00
To this you must add the cost to the employer of various items		
Employer's National Insurance (10.45% in 1990/91)		26.12
Canteen/luncheon voucher/subsistence allowances, say		7.00
Protective clothing and tools, say		1.88
Direct cost per employee	Weekly	£285.00
	× 52 = annual cost each	£14,820

Calculating a rate/hour to include overheads	£
Suppose you have 10 men whose annual cost is therefore	148,200
Suppose your overheads are similar to those in Example 2 but higher as this is a larger business. Let's also allow for a full-time receptionist/ secretary/book-keeper/general assistant, who is not charged out to each job, so we'll increase the £19,000 to, say	38,000
Add interest on loan or bank overdraft (or, if you owe nothing, a return on the money you put in yourself to finance the business), say	2,000
Add your own minimum earnings target – as per Example 1	20,800
Minimum turnover required	£209,000

which for 1,472 × 10 = 14,720 hours saleable = approx	£14.20/hr

But this does not allow for any 'super profit' or reward for the risk and responsibility of having your own business.

	£
Suppose you want a super profit of another £10,500: to earn that over 14,720 hours, you must add approx	0.68
	£14.88/hr
So you would round your labour rate to	£15.00/hr

You must work out your own rates per hour

Do not use the rates per hour in my examples. Work out your own after deciding:

- How much time you can sell.
- Whether the costs are realistic in your case.

Any variation in either of these factors could make a big difference to the rate per hour. For instance, any travel time to reach customers, which you cannot charge to them, has to come out of the allowance for unsold time, which you make when you assume you will sell 75 per cent, 70 per cent or whatever of your available hours.

And what will be *your* annual mileage in your car? Many people do far more than 10,000 miles a year on business.

Although the time sold is expressed in terms of weeks, this is the same thing as saying that, if you sell some time in *each* of the 46 available weeks, you will achieve an average per week of 34½ hours charged out if you sell 75 per cent, about 32 hours if you sell 70 per cent and so on.

What factors could alter the total cost per hour?

The £15.00 hourly rate depends upon the following factors:

- Proportion of chargeable time actually charged out.
- Number of people employed on chargeable work.
- Changes in wage costs.
- Changes in fixed costs.

A key assumption in the calculation of the hourly rate in Example 3 is that 80 per cent of the men's time during the 46 working weeks will be sold. Any variation from this will affect the cost.

If you do chargeable work yourself for some of the time, an estimate of that part of your time should be added to the figure for saleable hours. A similar proportion of your salary can then be included in direct costs.

When working out your own figures, try seeing how much the answer alters when you change an assumption about one of these factors. That will show you how sensitive your calculations are to errors in your estimates.

How much 'super profit' should I aim for?

In deciding how much 'super profit' to aim for, take into account how risky the business is – more people go bust in the building trade than in most others, for instance – and how much capital you have tied up in it which would earn you interest if it were in the bank.

Don't be swayed too much by your competitors' prices. Many businesses bankrupt themselves trying to undercut the rest. Price is only one factor in a customer's decision as to who he buys from. Quality, reliability and getting the job done on time are often just as important to him. For more on this point, see Chapter 18.

Poor control of time will destroy your profitability

Taking the figures calculated in Example 1, to budget for 70 per cent of time sold gives a rate per hour of £20.55 for 1,280 hours. But if you achieve only 65 per cent of time sold – 1,200 hours – you have lost 80 hours at £20.55 = £1,644. On planned sales of £26,300, that makes a hole of about 6.3 per cent.

Another way of looking at it is that you ought to have charged £21.92 per hour, the rate corresponding to 65 per cent efficiency.

If you budget for 65 per cent at £21.92 and achieve 70 per cent, you gain 80 hours at £21.92 = £1,754, which raises your sales by 6.7 per cent to £28,054.

These losses or profits may seem marginal but remember that they are at the top end of what you earn so their true significance is their impact on your net spending money.

Suppose you net £20,800 minimum but budget to earn £25,000 so as to gain a 'super profit' or true reward of £4,200 in return for the risk and responsibility of your own business. Your budgeted sales in Example 1 would have to be £30,500. A

£2,000 shortfall because of not controlling your time properly is only 6.6 per cent of that £30,500 but it cuts the real reward of £4,200 by nearly 50 per cent!

Don't treat your costings as inviolate

The labour rates produced by all these calculations should not be interpreted rigidly as meaning that work is unacceptable at a lower figure. They are a guide, a basis for making a judgement only. If you need work but can only get it at £15 per hour, you may have to take it at that rate. Some income is better than none. The decision should be based upon your position at that time. If you obtain work substantially above your hoped for average rate next time, you may still reach your target for the year.

Thus your pricing policy must be flexible. Perhaps work at £25 per hour can be obtained at certain times of the year, while jobs have to be accepted at £15 at other times.

Materials

Materials are omitted from these calculations because profit is not normally earned upon them. They are part of the costs of the job to be added to your price for your labour.

If you do make a profit on, say, spare parts, you should estimate the cost of what you use during the year. You can then easily calculate the contribution to your profits by applying your normal mark-up to that total. This gives you the amount of the margin you will earn. Since there will be costs – even if you hold no stocks there are bound to be some expenses to eat into that margin – it is best to regard it as an addition to the profit you make selling your time rather than enabling you to reduce the amount you need to charge for that time.

Costing records

Costing records for each job are vital to controlling your business. Whether or not you show labour charges separately from materials on your invoices, you should have a breakdown in your job records. These should show, job by job, the materials or parts used on it and the time spent on it. Then you can compare the actual results of particular jobs with the costings of them.

This is an essential discipline. It shows you where you make or lose money and provides valuable information upon which to plan your business.

Finally a cautionary tale about pricing too low as told to the *Financial Times*.

A young veterinary surgeon, eager to make a name for himself and therefore happy to turn out at all hours, drove out to an isolated farm one night in answer to an 'emergency' call. Arriving at the holding and asking to be led to the ailing beast, he was told there was no veterinary crisis.

'I have to get into town in a hurry,' the farmer said. 'My car's broken down and your visiting fee is less than the mini-cab fare.'

If you charge too little, people will abuse your time too!

Questions

- What are your own figures for:
  (a) Time available?
  (b) Expected proportion of time sold?
  (c) Costs?
- Using the principles explained in this chapter, what should be your rate per hour?

Chapter 17

Pricing Your Product

The previous chapter dealt with how to arrive at the price per hour to charge for your time. This one explains how to fix a price for a product you make.

There are two ways to approach the problem:

What does it cost me to make? *Or*
What is the most the customer will pay me for it?

It is important to charge as much as the market will bear. Underpricing can mean a business failure. The next chapter discusses why.

However, most people have to begin by working out what the product will cost to produce. Especially if it is a new idea, it may be difficult to know what people will pay for it.

The trouble with the question, 'How much does it cost to make?' is that there is no one answer. It depends on various factors. For example, it usually gets cheaper the more you produce so you need to know how many.

Then it also depends on which expenses you regard as part of the cost of production and which are just general overheads.

In theory one can divide costs into direct ones which vary more or less in ratio with the quantity produced, and fixed costs which stay much the same, whether you make a few or a lot.

The materials used in the product are an obvious direct cost. The rent of the factory is a fixed cost – until the next rent review, anyway.

Sadly, life is not so simple. Take materials. They do not vary directly! Why not? The reasons differ according to the business. In a factory, the wastage in warming up or changing over machines tends to be similar, whether it is a short or a long run, so longer runs reduce the waste per unit. With long runs, production workers become more practised, thus also reducing wastage, and output is higher because less time is taken up in changing from product to product on the machines.

In a small business, purchase prices for materials tend to be high because the orders placed with suppliers are small. Moreover, if you have to place orders of a minimum size, small sizes mean left-over quantities of materials or part-made goods lying about your premises which usually deteriorate or perhaps become unusable because of changes in demand. This is a big risk in a fashion business, for instance. Increase the throughput and you buy cheaper while reducing your wastage.

So the problem often is that one cannot work out the *direct* cost per unit without first deciding the quantity one expects to sell. As for the *fixed* costs, they obviously vary even more according to the quantity. For example, if your fixed costs are £40,000 a year for rent, rates, telephone, depreciation etc, the amount per unit for a sale of 20,000 units is £2 but double that if you think you will shift only 10,000 units.

How marginal costing can help you

Marginal costing sounds like a horrible piece of accounting jargon but its meaning is simple and very important. Variable costs alter with sales volume. Fixed costs do not. An order at a price which covers all variable costs and contributes something towards fixed costs may be worth having even though the price is low.

A department or product may be worth keeping even though it apparently does not cover its fixed costs. Marginal costing seeks to identify such situations.

How a potter could profit from a big order at a low price

The potter makes mugs. His costs are as follows:

	£
Rent and rates	6,000
Electricity	3,000
Motor expenses	2,000
Telephone, stationery etc	1,000
	£12,000

For practical purposes these costs do not alter however many mugs he makes. Of course his electricity bill will increase as he uses his equipment more but the alteration in cost of electricity per mug will not be significant over a range of production volumes.

Suppose his cost of materials per mug is 80p and his average sales are 217 mugs per week in the 46 weeks available to him annually: say, 10,000 mugs a year. His fixed costs of £12,000 pa are thus £1.20 per mug. With materials his total cost per mug is £2. If he sells at £3.20 each he has a profit of £1.20 each or £12,000 pa.

Marginal cost of the potter
His marginal cost is 80p per pot, ie the cost for materials per pot which changes directly according to the number he makes.

Can the potter take a big order at a low price?
A customer offers him an order for 4,000 mugs at £2.60 only. He can make the mugs without prejudicing other sales but his total cost of £2 per mug leaves him a profit per unit halved to 60p on this order. Is this correct thinking? How does he decide whether or not to take the order?

New fixed cost per mug
If, for the same fixed costs of £12,000, he now makes 14,000 mugs, his fixed cost per mug is 85.7p – say 86p.

New profit calculation
The position then is:

	£
He sells 10,000 mugs at £3.20	32,000
He sells 4,000 mugs at £2.60	10,400
Total sales 14,000	42,400
Less: variable cost of materials	
14,000 at 80p	11,200
Fixed costs	12,000
Net profit	£19,200

Why is net profit up by 60 per cent from £12,000 to £19,200?
His extra profit is made up thus:

	£
4,000 mugs sold at profit of 94p (£2.60 − 80p − 86p)	3,760
10,000 mugs sold at profit of £1.54 (£3.20 − 80p − 86p)	15,400
Differences because of rounding up cost to 86p	40
Net profit: £1.37 per mug on average	£19,200

Thus he made less profit per mug on the big order but the increased production meant that his fixed costs per mug were £1.20 − 86p = 34p lower. His overall profit per mug was thus 17p higher even though he took the big order at a cut price.

High volume equals low fixed costs

In fact the potter could make more money by taking an order at any price which covered his materials cost and made some contribution towards his fixed costs. However, if you are in a similar position, don't take my example too literally. I have oversimplified the kind of situation usually found in business. For one thing fixed costs tend to increase a little with higher volume. You can't run machines for extra hours without eventually increasing the repair bills, for instance. Then if you set too low a price for a volume order, it may make it more difficult for your other customers to sell and thus reduce your sales to them.

Also if you cut prices too far, you could find you end up working harder to produce more goods at lower profits per item and that, after paying your fixed costs, you make no more profit!

Another danger is that you increase your sales volume to a point at which you cannot meet your orders without extending your facilities, thus increasing your fixed costs and making some of your lower priced deals unprofitable. More about this later.

Nevertheless, the principle is that high volume reduces fixed costs per unit and often makes for higher profits in spite of lower prices. This may seem to conflict with the idea that you must charge the highest price you can get which is explained in the next chapter. The point is that, when fixing your ordinary price, you must set it high. Then, if someone offers you a big order, you can do the arithmetic to see whether it is worth taking at the price offered.

Another point about pricing a product or service

If your product or service has a high variable cost, a price increase may raise profits in spite of lower volume sales. The reverse applies if the variable cost is low: Thus:

		Before		After	
Product or service		A	B	A	B
Sales 100 units at £1		£100	£100		
Raise prices by 10%:					
Volume falls by 15%					
so 85 at £1.10				£93.50	£93.50
Variable cost	60% for A	£60		85 at 60p	£51.00	
	30% for B		£30	85 at 30p		£25.50
Contribution		£40	£70	£42.50	£68.00

For a 10 per cent price rise and a 15 per cent sales fall the contribution goes up for the product with the high variable cost/low contribution but down for the one with the low variable cost/high contribution. Now calculate the effect of a price reduction of 10 per cent. What increase in volume is needed to earn the same contribution that each product earns at £1?

	A	B
Selling price is now	90p	90p
Contribution per unit is 40p – 10p	30p	
70p – 10p		60p
Total contribution wanted to maintain profits	£40	£70
No of unit sales required (£40 ÷ 30p: £70 ÷ 60p)	133	117
An increase of	33.3%	17%

Thus you need to understand the relationship of prices, costs and sales volumes for your products or services if you are to make the best decisions on how much to charge. Beware of distorting the facts by the arbitrary division of costs. Let's see what that means.

A more complicated costing situation with three products

Suppose you have three products. You analyse your accounts to show the following position:

162

		Total		A		B		C
	%	£	%	£	%	£	%	£
Sales		100,000		60,000		30,000		10,000
Gross profit (contribution to fixed costs)	15	15,000	10	6,000	20	6,000	30	3,000
Fixed costs (divided in proportion to sales)	12	12,000	12	7,200	12	3,600	12	1,200
Net profit (Loss)	3	£3,000	(2)	(£1,200)	8	£2,400	18	£1,800

Net profit is poor. What action do you take? Do you cut out product A because it appears to make a loss?

Cut out product A
Suppose you promote product C hard because of its high gross profit. You double its sales and stop selling product A. The position is then:

		Total		B		C
	%	£	%	£	%	£
Sales		50,000		30,000		20,000
Gross profit (contribution to fixed costs)	24	12,000	20	6,000	30	6,000
Fixed costs (in proportion to sales)	24	12,000	24	7,200	24	4,800
		Nil	(4)	(£1,200)	6	£1,.200

Where has all the profit gone?
You cut out a loss-making product. You pushed hard the one making the highest profit and doubled its sales. This decisive action has resulted in your losing what little profit you had. Why?

Do not allocate costs arbitrarily
The answer lies in the fixed costs. The gross profit is a contribution to those costs. Product A contributed £6,000 towards them. The loss of £1,200 on product A was a notional one only. Such nonsense figures result from the obsession of accountants with allocating costs which should not be allocated. There was no logical basis for splitting the fixed costs in proportion to sales. It was convenient but it had no relevance to the business situation.

The real position was a total contribution by the three products of £15,000 towards the fixed costs of £12,000. Cutting out product A did not reduce the fixed costs. Since the increased contribution by product C from its extra sales was only £3,000 the loss of £6,000 from product A eliminated the net profit. The real problem was not the theoretical 'loss' made on A but how to increase the total gross profit or contribution towards fixed costs and profit made by all three products.

Limitations upon marginal costing

Marginal costing is a useful technique. Like all techniques it must not be misused. Business decisions are not usually as simple as in the above examples but the idea that one should not arbitrarily apportion fixed costs is an important one. The key is to maximise the *contribution* made by your products towards your fixed costs and profit. So long as a product makes a contribution, it should be retained until you reach your sales capacity. At that point, it may pay to drop it to make room for a more profitable one rather than invest in expanding your capacity.

Again, the example above is oversimplified to make the point. The gross profit on a product is only the same as the contribution it makes if there are no other costs of selling, distribution etc which relate to it specifically. For instance, some products may be more expensive to sell. Your measurements of contribution should take account of such differences.

Will you need extra investment if you take that big order?

Big orders at low prices often mean that extra equipment to increase capacity has to be bought, thus raising costs. If you raise your unit sales higher than your factory can produce, by accepting extra business at low prices, you may find that what was profitable when you had spare capacity now loses you money. The reason will be that your fixed costs have gone up because of the need to increase capacity by buying new machines or extending the factory and that the margin on those extra orders does not cover the increase in fixed costs required to service them.

When you reach your production capacity consider restricting sales at low prices or cutting out less profitable products. Do not automatically take on extra business at cut prices. Consider the whole picture.

Maximising profit is the aim

The object is to maximise profit, not sales. If your shop or factory is overstretched, it may pay you to cut out your least profitable activities but only if you have correctly measured the variable costs (marginal cost) relating to them.

Sometimes an unprofitable product or activity is a 'loss leader' which brings in other good business and has to be retained for that reason.

Beware of high margin lines

To maximise profit it is tempting to push the high margin lines which show the greatest contribution. But this can be a false trail. High margins often go with low volume. Better profits may result from promoting lines with average margins but volume sales potential.

Questions

- What is the principle of marginal costing? Check your answer with the text.
- You make wooden crates. The cost of materials used for each crate is £2 and the direct labour costs you £3 in wages. Last year's sales were 50,000 crates. Your overhead costs, including your own pay, were £75,000.
  - (a) What was your total cost per crate? Marginal cost per crate?
  - (b) A new customer offers you an order for 10,000 crates at £6.
    Do you take it?
    What points do you consider when deciding?
  - (c) You find that you can only handle the business if you increase your overhead costs by £15,000 pa. Do you take the order?
- You have three products. Their selling prices and other figures are as follows:

Product	A	B	C
Selling price	£1	£4	£6
Gross margin (%)	20%	30%	15%
Quantity sold	8,000	3,000	3,000
Total floor space			
1,000 sq ft			

Floor space occupied (%)	25%	35%	40%
Stocks held (based on cost, remember)	8 weeks	12 weeks	3 weeks

1. What is the proportion of total sales which each product produces?

   What is the proportion of the total gross margin which each product contributes?

   What are the sales per square foot for each product?

   What is the gross profit per square foot for each product?

   What is the stock value for each product?

   What is the order of profitability of the products based on:
   - space usage?
   - investment in stock?

2. If your space were limited, which product would you cut down on and which would you promote?

   If you were short of cash, to which product would you give most attention and which would you promote?

Answers

The wooden crates

(a) Total cost per crate   £6.50

      Marginal cost per crate   £5.00

(b) You take the order provided that you can handle it within your existing capacity without increasing your costs.

      You consider the possible effects on the market price for your crates if others hear of the low price and you look carefully for any extra cost involved. On the other hand, you look for possible reductions in materials and direct labour per crate resulting from 20 per cent higher throughput.

(c) You do not take the order if you will have to increase your overheads by £15,000. The order would contribute £1 per crate or £10,000 towards overheads so you would lose £5,000.

The three products

All percentages to nearest whole.

		Total		A		B		C
Product sales		£38,000		£8,000		£12,000		£18,000
Proportion of sales		100%		21%		32%		47%
Cost of sales		£30,100		£6,400		£8,400		£15,300
Gross profit	21%	£7,900	20%	£1,600	30%	£3,600	15%	£2,700
Gross margin contributed (%)		100%		20%		46%		34%
Floor space occupied (%)		100%		25%		35%		40%
Floor area used in sq ft		1,000		250		350		400
Sales per sq ft		£38		£32		£34		£45
Gross profit per sq ft		£7.90		£6.40		£10.30		£6.75
Stock value (based on cost of sales)	$\frac{6.6}{52}$	£3,800	$\frac{8}{52}$	£980	$\frac{12}{52}$	£1,940	$\frac{3}{52}$	£880

Note how misleading the sales and gross profit percentages are as a guide to true profitability. Gross profit per square foot shows quite a different order of merit from sales per square foot. Note also how the totals conceal wide variations between the products.

Product B earns most gross profit per square foot and so would be promoted, with product C taking second place if space was short.

Product C requires the least investment in stock. It is a low margin, fast moving line of high unit value – such as cigarettes. Product B is a high margin line requiring stocks to service sales. A cash shortage could be helped by a careful review of the stocks held for product B. As B is the largest investment in stock, a small improvement will have the greatest effect.

The danger of reducing stocks of B is that sales might suffer. This could be serious because of the high gross profit per square foot of space. However, customers might accept some element of waiting time – this is probably not a product bought on impulse.

Let's see how the figures might work out:

Suppose the stocks of B can be cut by 10 per cent.
This releases cash of   £194
It also releases floor space of 35 sq ft.
Suppose this space can be used for a new line at the same profit margin as C.
Assume that stocks of the new line are in the same proportion of stocks to floor area as C so new stock absorbs
thus: £880 ÷ 400 sq ft = £2.2 × 35 sq ft   £77

Net cash released from stocks   £117

167

If sales of B fall by 5 per cent as a result of reduced stocks

Reduction is £600 @ gross profit of 30 per cent.	£180
Suppose the stocks of new product represent 3 weeks' usage as for C.	
Usage is then 77 ÷ 3 × 52 = £1,335	
Grossed up the usage for a gross profit of 15 per cent	
suggests sales of £1,570 and gross profit of:	£235
Gross profit increase	£55

This exercise shows you how, given some simple assumptions, you can work out the financial results of changing the way the business works. It is of course a theoretical example based on simple suppositions and using small figures, but it demonstrates the scope for profit improvement by management able to use financial information properly.

Never, however, make decisions based on figures alone. All figures are based on assumptions and assumptions are often either guesses or crude estimates. Always check with the people affected by the new policy to see if there are reasons why either the assumptions are inaccurate or why the theory won't work in practice.

Chapter 18

Why You Ought to Charge a Lot for What You Do

In the previous two chapters I have shown you how to arrive at the *minimum* price you can afford to sell at. Now here's some more about the importance of charging the *highest* price you can get.

Most businesses have some choice over their prices

There are more businesses which have a choice between charging a high or a low price than you might think. Although wholesalers and retailers mostly cannot charge more than the manufacturer's suggested prices and often have to discount them, even they have a choice of *how much* discount to offer.

An example of a trade with no fixed prices is cosmetics. Although pots of face cream tend to cost much the same to make, they sell for widely differing prices depending upon the marketing policy and image of the manufacturer. This being a dreams and illusions market, each maker must decide how he wishes to position himself in the public eye. The image options range from good value, no frills preparations to super luxury, top priced exclusivity. Only at the bottom end does price top the list of consumer reasons for purchase, if indeed it does then. The more expensive brands must first establish an image of quality, reliability and style as selling points and heavy marketing expenditure is necessary to do this. Prices are, of course, influenced by the competition in the particular section of the market in which the manufacturer wishes to compete but they are not the key selling point.

As a contrast, take a baked beans manufacturer who sells a product roughly the same as anyone else's. In theory he cannot deviate much from the usual price per can. In practice, even he has some scope for improving his prices by careful negotiation to restrict the discounts for quantity, which the big retailers demand from him.

Another type of market is for a technical product which sells

169

on performance. A factory machine or an office photocopier, for instance, probably has several apparent competitors. However, these are likely to vary considerably in their precise capabilities, mode of operation etc, and the customer's buying decision is often based on these points with the price a secondary consideration (within limits, naturally). And, of course, a new product may have no directly comparable competition at all. The first desk calculators, for example, gave business executives a new tool. Previously the only means of doing one-off calculations were slide rules, which were slow, and comptometers, which required trained operators.

Some types of service are highly price competitive but many others are not as much as they appear to be. A launderette or a window cleaner may in theory be constrained by the prices others charge, but even they can justify and obtain more than average if they offer a better service.

In many cases, particularly when the customer is another business, it is quality and speed of service which come before price.

Get the best price you can

Fixing your prices is one of the most important business decisions you'll make! If you have a choice you must charge the highest price you can get. To see why, let's take the example of a new product you've developed for which there is no competition at the moment – or at least nothing directly comparable.

Suppose it is not an exclusive luxury product and you therefore hope to get volume sales. Indeed you probably need to in order to make a profit at the low price which would make the product easy to sell.

The temptation is to pitch the initial price low. That's usually a mistake. If you can spend a lot of money on advertising and promotion, you may get the volume you need. If not you're probably only going to sell a few at first no matter how low the price. Why? Because no one knows you, no one knows your product. It's a new idea and people need time to accept new ideas.

If you sell direct, you will have to keep repeating your advertising and your mail shots or salesmen's visits to prospective customers. You will need sales literature and must pay either heavy postage costs for mailing shots to prospects or provide brochures, together with sales aids such as samples or mock-ups, to your salesmen. The latter will want cars if they are full time. Even if you use part-time agents, they need supporting and administering.

If you sell through retailers it won't be easy or quick getting them to stock and display your wondrous idea, let alone explain it properly to prospective buyers.

One way or another, it will take you time and cost you a bomb to get the message to your potential customers. Sales will be slower than you hoped and will cost more to get than you budgeted for. Charging a high price may help to sell the idea by giving it an exclusive image. It will allow you to give a better commission to those who sell for you, whether salesmen or retailers, thus making it more rewarding for them. And the higher margin per unit will usually give you more profit out of which to finance your marketing. Remember you are unlikely to sell a lot whatever you do. Runaway successes in new ideas are few. Most take time and hard graft to get established so a good profit on the sales you do achieve is vital.

If I sound over-pessimistic about your chances, remember that the above has been the story of many good ideas. The failure rate is high and even those which survive often do not produce anywhere near the hoped-for rewards to their originators because they are marketed too cheaply. High prices will enable you to pay for the marketing expenses necessary to sell the product or service. They provide a cushion to cope with the inevitable unforeseen costs. Once sales start to build up, they provide the cash necessary to plough back to improve the product, develop the market and to finance expansion.

Resist the temptation to set the lowest price you can for fear of the customer. Price up and then use the additional profit to market aggressively, to show off and publicise your product or service. If it is any good and you have allowed yourself enough cash for marketing, you'll find enough selling points to attract buyers.

You are never going to sell to every potential purchaser anyway. Many sales will be stymied by reasons outside your control such as established connections elsewhere, wrong person approached, too much of another product in stock, or he's just feeling like saying 'no'; there are umpteen reasons why your sales approach will fail in a proportion of cases whatever you do. Of course, you will overcome many of them, either by persistence or by correcting your own mistakes, but this costs money and takes time.

Your price will always be too high for some people no matter how low you set it. Forget them. Set a figure to give you a really good margin. If your product or service and your marketing approach are adequate you will find enough customers to more than pay for the ones you lose on price.

Once you've got going, the initial high price enables you either to make cuts as your competitors catch up and copy you, or to finance the research necessary to stay one jump ahead technically.

An example of the arithmetic of high prices

Direct variable cost per unit of your product (cost of sales)	£10
Other costs which do not vary directly with each unit (selling, advertising, administration etc)	£60,000

How many units must be sold to cover fixed costs if price is £20?
Answer. Fixed costs must be met from margin after paying variable costs.
So £60,000 divided by the gross profit (£20 − £10 = £10); so breakeven is   6,000 units

	£
say 6,000 units sell at £20	120,000
Cost of sales at £10 each × 6,000 = direct costs	60,000
Break-even point: gross profit equals the other costs	60,000

Suppose that you could have obtained £24 per unit without loss of sales. The arithmetic is then:

6,000 units at £24	144,000
Cost of sales at £10	60,000
Other costs	60,000
Profit	£24,000

Or looking at it another way, the break-even point is now £60,000 divided by £14 (the new gross margin) = 4,286 units, a considerable reduction from 6,000.

Now let's compare the results over the next three years for the two prices assuming:
(a) Selling prices stay the same at £20 and £24.
(b) Initial sales 8,000 units.
(c) Growth in sales of 25 per cent per year.

(d) Variable costs stay the same, the cost per unit being held down by the rising number of units sold.
(e) Other costs rise by 10 per cent.
(f) You take out a salary of £20,000, then £22,000 then £26,000.

Year	Sales Prices		Sales units	Gross margin		Fixed costs	Salary	Net profit	
	A	B		at £10	at £14			A	B
				A	B				
	£	£		£	£	£	£	£	£
1	20	24	8,000	80,000	112,000	60,000	20,000	Nil	32,000
2	20	24	10,000	100,000	140,000	66,000	22,000	12,000	52,000
3	20	24	12,500	125,000	175,000	72,600	26,000	26,400	76,400
						Total profit		£38,400	£160,400

Startled by the arithmetic? A 20 per cent increase in price more than quadruples the net profit earned over three years! At or near break-even point, a price increase has a dramatic effect on profits, as you can see. The arithmetical ratio of the higher profits to the lower ones then decreases each year but this is misleading. The extra profit rises from £32,000 to £40,000, then £50,000.

Why is it so important to earn good profits?

The answer has nothing to do with politics or the fair distribution of wealth. Such considerations only start to apply when high *disposable* profits are earned. Usually with a new company or a new product, the extra profit is not disposable; it is badly needed to pay back money borrowed for the project, to finance expansion or to provide the extra working capital needed for the growing level of sales.

Let's calculate the working capital needed to finance a manufacturer on the basis of the figures in this example. We'll assume that debtors (accounts receivable) and stocks of materials and finished goods each represent six weeks' sales and that creditors (accounts payable) allow four weeks' credit for purchases. To keep it simple, we'll ignore VAT which, if applicable to sales, increases the debtor balances and is payable on many purchase and expense invoices, thus inflating creditors too.

At £20 and £24 per unit, sales in year 3 will be £250,000 and £300,000. Assuming that sales rise steadily throughout the period, weekly turnover might be £5,500 and £6,600 (both 275 units) at the end of the third year.

The working capital needed by the end of year 3 will then be as follows:

	Low price £	High price £
Debtors will be the final six weeks' sales	33,000	39,600
Stocks at cost (275 units × 6 × £10 for both)	16,500	16,500
	49,500	56,100
Less financed by creditors: four weeks' purchases (275 units × 4 × £10 plus, say, £3,000 fixed costs)	14,000	14,000
Working capital required by end of year 3.	£35,500	£42,100

Comparing these figures with the net profits calculated above shows that the low price will not generate enough cash to finance the business. The working capital figure does not include anything for expenditure on fixed assets, such as equipment or premises, while the profits shown earlier are before paying tax. On the other hand, the high price will handsomely cover the immediate needs leaving the balance to invest in the future by buying new equipment, launching a bigger marketing campaign or whatever.

I have shown you a simplified version of real life, in order to make the key points clear.

If your product is new and without competition, it is only a matter of time before someone else copies you. You need profits to pay for research on technical improvements to keep you ahead. A high starting price may, of course, stimulate competition but it also give you the scope to reduce your prices when the newcomers undercut you: by then you will be established while they will still be learning the ropes with all the attendant start-up costs and they will not find it easy to retaliate.

The extra profit makes all the difference to the company

To summarise, set your prices as high as you dare. In many situations a better price can be obtained for the sacrifice of relatively few sales. Remember it is easier to reduce prices than to increase them.

The extra profit obtainable from correctly pricing a product or service is likely to make all the difference to the future of the business. It provides self-generated cash to finance expansion, further development of the product or to pay for new facilities. It may enable you to avoid further borrowings, which are difficult and expensive for a young company to obtain, and to pay back existing loans.

For the owners it means that they stay in charge because they can continue to finance development. They are not forced to sell out to a large organisation or to restrict growth.

For the employees it means a larger cake out of which can come the money for better working conditions and the investment in new plant, more research etc which will keep the company in business a few years hence, ie good profits mean job security. Only when there is money to meet all the future needs of the business is the surplus truly disposable. Then it may be a matter of politics or social justice that some of it be distributed elsewhere than the owner's pocket. Until you reach that happy position, high prices are essential to your business survival.

Chapter 19

Why Budget?

In earlier sections I have explained:

- What your annual accounts tell you and how they can help you to control your business.
- How to use the records you already have to manage your finances from day to day.

The third element of financial control is a budget for the future. Thus:

- Annual accounts tell you where you are now.
- Budgets say where you want to go.
- Routine financial control makes sure you get there.

That suggests I ought to have explained budgets before looking at day-to-day controls, but I have left the budget until now for several reasons. A budget takes time to prepare and may seem a daunting task if you have not done one before. In contrast, many of the basic financial controls already explained can be introduced quickly and with the minimum of effort.

If you did not have those controls in place, you were not managing your finances as well as you might have been; indeed, you probably lacked the habit of financial discipline. If so, you would have been unlikely to accept the idea of preparing a budget. I hope that I have persuaded you to make some changes and that you have discovered that good control of money is not difficult and can make a major contribution to ensuring your success.

Moreover, if you lack the basic financial controls you need to get a grip on your short-term finances, you will not have some of the information you need to do a proper budget. That's why I have explained those controls first.

I keep saying how important these controls are if you are to minimise the amount of money tied up in your business. In the next section I will prove it in figures, at the same time showing you how to use a budget to help you plan ahead. First, here are a few points about what a budget is and is not, and why it is so valuable.

A budget is a key part of the financial control system. Profitable businesses need financial control to make sure they stay profitable. Expanding ones must have it to ensure that the extra sales are profitable and that money is available to exploit opportunities for growth. If you are making a loss, financial control is about maximising your chances of survival. A budget helps to run any business.

What does a budget do?

It helps you to guess what is probably going to happen before it does and therefore to do something about it. Thus it helps you to influence, even control, your future instead of just letting it happen to you.

The budget estimates your sales, expenses and profits. It forecasts how much profit will be tied up in equipment, stocks, debtors etc, and how much will be in cash available for spending as you wish.

How can I budget when I don't know my sales?

This is a familiar cry of managers who look for an excuse not to budget. But, as we shall see, the sales level assumed does not usually matter very much, provided it is worked out on a sensible basis of comparison with last year, new products introduced etc. Of course, you do not know how long the grass will grow next year. But you *do* know that it will grow and that, on average, you will have to cut it every week. Since you know the capacity and speed of your mowing machine you can estimate how long it will take to cut and roughly how much petrol you will use. This is only a guess but it gives you enough to work on.

To write down plans and to express them in money terms as a budget is a great aid to clear thinking. Putting things in writing helps to identify problems in advance. You can see the effect of different policies and understand the key points of your business finances.

Later, as sales and costs alter, you can use your budget to judge in advance the impact of the changes on your profits. Even the smallest business runs better on a budget. It is like your personal affairs: if you did not work to any plan at all, you would soon have no money left.

A budget, any budget, even the most simple unsophisticated plan, helps you to foresee problems – which helps to prevent them – and to forecast the consequences thus enabling you to minimise the losses. On the other side of the coin, it helps you to spot the opportunities and be ready to exploit them.

A budget is not a panacea

A budget helps to light the way ahead. It is not a precise forecast; it is your best estimate. But that estimate is so much more likely to come true because it is based on logical thought and on plans, which have been proved to work on paper. A paper plan is still theory but at least it is logical theory; if you do it properly, you will spot the nonsenses, such as planning to sell 1000 Whizzwogs when you can only produce, or obtain, 900 of them.

Why can't I do it in my head?

'I already know my figures – I see them every day. I am constantly planning ahead – it's all up here', say so many businessmen tapping their heads. Sure you do – so do I in my business. But, whether we like it or not, we cannot carry it all 'up there'. Of course, we plan for sales, estimate our costs etc, but we do it less efficiently if it is all in our heads. It is too easy to miss something.

If you are one of those 'naturals' who prosper by the seat of their pants, good luck to you. But be warned that the truly brilliant are few in number; many come unstuck. It is easy to make money for a while from a good idea, particularly during a boom, but booms don't last and good ideas attract competition. The going always gets tough sooner or later and it's then that financial planning tells. It's no good if you cannot survive in the hard times as well as the good ones.

Equally, the problems get bigger as a business grows. Success often turns sour when growth outstrips the management's ability to control it.

Do you manage by crisis?

Many businesses stagger from crisis to crisis. They make profits all right; maybe they prosper but it is one panic after another! As soon as one is solved by urgent 'decisive' action, another crops up. So plans have to be continually adapted; everyone lives on their nerves and little or no sound development or long-term planning takes place. If it does, no one takes it seriously because they know there will be another crisis next week. Recognise the scene? Budgeting can help you to change it.

Budgets allow managers to manage

'Surely the budget will restrict my freedom to run my show – tie me down', say some managers. Not so! In fact, the managers of a business can be given more freedom once a budget has been agreed for the company. They can be left to get on with running their particular responsibilities within the limits of the budget. Their freedom to manage is the greater because it has been defined. Only when they wish to act outside the plan do they need to refer decisions upwards.

Don't use budgets as a stick!

You will only get the full benefit of the point above if you do, in fact, let your people manage. If you have a sensible reporting system tied to a budget, you will know as soon as anything important goes wrong. Meanwhile, let them get on with it. Some bosses try to use budgets as a means of putting pressure on people. This is silly since any manager worth his salt can fiddle his results for a while and such pressure usually defeats its object.

Use realistic objectives

Your budget objectives should be attainable, otherwise no one will take them seriously. You must be able to hold people responsible for attaining budget – this is not the same as using it to put pressure on them.

Use separate targets to stretch performance. Thus budget may be sales of 1000 Whizzwogs but target 1100, with bonuses etc for achieving this. Attaining target means exceeding budget with appropriate rewards. Failing to meet budget means poor performance and inquests accordingly.

Can the budget be changed?

The budget itself should only be changed during the year if really drastic and unforeseen alterations in circumstances occur, such as moving premises. The problem, if one changes the budget itself (as opposed to agreeing 'planned variances' on it), is that is becomes difficult to remember which figures are which budget, new or old, and confusion usually arises.

However, the budget is a tool of management, not a restriction on it. There is no reason why changes in forecasts should not be made, new policies adopted etc. Indeed, the budget helps you to do this. Forecasts, however, are outline statements giving the main headings only for sales, expenses etc, to give a new 'expected result'. This can be altered every week if you wish, but leave the original budget as it is and report against it, not against the forecast.

Why a budget will help you to succeed

Suppose you had to cross a desert. If you had a map, a compass and had worked out how much water you would need, you would have a much better chance of arriving at the other side than if you simply set forth and worked it out as you went along. The budget is the equivalent preparation in business. It cannot guarantee your success but it will much improve your prospects. Planning ahead reduces the risk by helping to identify problems before they occur.

Summary

The advantages of a budget are:

- It makes you think ahead, step outside the daily load of current problems.
- It identifies likely future difficulties, helps to forecast the consequences, helps you to cope.
- It helps you to identify the costs attributable to departments or activities.
- It helps you to fix your prices.

- It helps you to spot opportunities, forecast the results of different policies.
- It is a target which, when compared with actual results, gives an early warning that things are going wrong.
- It helps you to plan corrective action.
- It gives managers more freedom to manage, allows the boss to delegate.
- It reduces 'management by crisis' – perhaps the biggest bonus of all.

Budgets are not complicated and difficult to understand. The principles are simple. Anyone can master them with a little study. Work through the following chapter with me and you will see how you can start to budget for your business.

Chapter 20

An Example of a Simple Budget

In this chapter I demonstrate the importance of routine controls if you are to minimise the money tied up in your business. I ask you to fill in the figures yourself because doing it for yourself is the best way to learn.

In working through the example you will be revising your understanding of the previous chapters. If in doubt on any point, check back to the relevant part of the book. Once you have completed the example, you will have done a budget!

Prudent and Carefree

Two contracting businesses, Prudent and Carefree, offer the same service. Their main cost is wages though they also use some materials. This is their first year of trading so the sales and profits are small. This is realistic because many new businesses barely break even or lose money in year one. If the figures seem small to you, add a nought or two mentally. The principles are exactly the same whatever the size of the numbers.

The task is to prepare a budget filling in the blank profit and loss account, balance sheet and source and application of funds statement on the following pages. The necessary information is given in the text.

All you have to do is enter the figures I give you on the blank forms. I'm not asking you to do any accounting work and only a little calculation where one figure is derived from another. In working out the figures you will be producing a simple budget, just as you might for your own business.

You will also see for yourself how important the financial control of stock, debtors and creditors is and how failure to exercise that control along the lines discussed previously in the book can prejudice the survival of your business.

You will see that Carefree makes various mistakes and the exercise shows you their effect in comparison with Prudent's figures.

Round your figures and work in pencil

Round all figures to the nearest £100 where necessary. Round up £50, for example. This speeds up the additions and simplifies the schedules. Work in pencil so that you can alter your figures easily.

Profit and loss account information

Use this information to fill in the profit and loss account. Do it now rather than go on reading. Fill in each figure as you come to it.

Sales
£100,000 for both businesses. This is the expected sales figure. It is based on the best available information but, especially for a new business, it often has to be a 'guesstimate'.

Materials
Both businesses include materials in their costings of their contracts at 25 per cent of sales. Carefree, however, experiences stock wastage in addition of £1,000. Since you have an estimate of the sales, these assumptions allow you to work out the materials cost.

Cash discounts
Prudent pays his suppliers promptly and obtains 2½ per cent discount on his purchases of materials. Round your calculated sum to the nearest £100. It will be a deduction and therefore shown in brackets.

Wages
Both businesses include 8,000 hours of work in their costing of contracts at a wages cost of £6 per hour. Carefree fails to control his workforce, however, and 250 hours of extra overtime (3.1 per cent of target hours) are worked at £8 per hour. These figures allow you to work out the wages bill.

Gross profit
This is, of course, sales less materials and wages.

Prudent and Carefree
Profit and loss account for year to 31 December
Year 1

	Prudent		Carefree	
	%	£	%	£
Sales				
Materials				
Cash discounts obtained (2½% on materials)				
Wages				
Cost of sales				
Gross profit				
Total expenses				
Bank interest (at 15%)				
Depreciation: plant and equipment				
Net profit	%	£	%	£
Re-stated as				
Proprietor's salary				
Super profit				
		£		£

Expenses
£12,000 for both businesses. I do not give you the detail because it does not matter for the purpose of this example but the total covers overheads, such as rent, insurance, motor expenses, telephone and stationery.

Bank interest
£500 for Prudent but £1,200 for Carefree. Normally you would not be able to calculate interest at this stage. You would have to go on to do the budgeted balance sheet in order to see how much money would be borrowed, on which interest would be payable. I have already done this to make it easy for you to do the example.

The interest figures are low in relation to the overdrafts, but I have assumed that the capital introduced by each owner covered the initial expenditure on fixed assets. The sales increased in the second six months to over double the first half total, so working capital needs will have been much lower to start with than at the end of the year. Thus the overdrafts for much of the year will have been much lower than at the balance sheet date.

Depreciation of plant and equipment
£1,000 for both businesses.

Net profit
You should now be able to calculate this.

Proprietor's notional salary
When restating the profit, take this as £13,000 for both businesses. Do not confuse the notional salary with the owner's actual drawings which will be mentioned later. You will find that Carefree has a notional super loss.

Balance sheet information

Fixed assets
These are the same for both businesses.

Plant and equipment
£5,000 owned at start of year depreciated at 20 per cent.

Vehicles
£6,000 owned at start of year depreciated at 25 per cent.

You can calculate the depreciation on plant and equipment from the above, though we have already come across it as a figure in the profit and loss account. That on motor vehicles is included in the expenses total of £12,000.

Prudent and Carefree
Balance sheet as at 31 December
Year 1

	Cost	Accumulated depreciation	Prudent Net book value	Carefree Net book value
Fixed assets	£	£	£	£
Plant and equipment				
Vehicles	____	____	____	____
	____	____		
Current assets				
Stock				
Debtors (remember VAT!)				
Payments in advance			____	____
Total current assets			____	____
Total assets				
Current liabilities due within one year				
Creditors (remember VAT!)				
VAT payable				
Bank overdraft			____	____
Total current liabilities			____	____
Proprietor's interest			£ ____	£ ____
Represented by:				
Capital introduced at start of year				
Add profit for the year (before tax)			____	____
Less drawings (actual cash drawn, not notional 'salary')				____
			£ ____	£ ____

Analysis of sales and materials usage
You will need the figures below to work out stocks, debtors and creditors in the next few steps. The figures do not include VAT.

Current assets
Round to nearest £100. Do not forget to adjust for VAT at 15 per cent. Take all months as 30 days and use the monthly analysis opposite to calculate stocks and debtors.

	Prudent	Carefree
Stocks: No of days' usage of materials	30 days	45 days
Debtors: No of days' sales	45 days	60 days
Payments in advance	£500	£500

| | Sales | Materials usage | |
| | | Prudent | Carefree |
		25%	26%
Jan	2,000	500	500
Feb	2,000	500	500
Mar	4,000	1,000	1,100
Apr	5,000	1,250	1,250
May	6,000	1,500	1,600
Jun	8,000	2,000	2,100
Jul	11,000	2,750	2,850
Aug	10,000	2,500	2,600
Sep	12,000	3,000	3,100
Oct	14,000	3,500	3,600
Nov	14,000	3,500	3,700
Dec	12,000	3,000	3,100
	£100,000	£25,000	£26,000

Warning! There is a trap for you in these ratios! Before you jump to a conclusion as to how to use the figures to calculate your answers, pause to consider whether it gives you a figure which means anything, given the monthly trend of the numbers. Are you applying the ratio of the number of days, one, one and a half or two months to the figures to which they relate?

Current liabilities
Round to nearest £100. Assume VAT at 15 per cent.

	Prudent	Carefree
Creditors:		
Trade: Usage of materials	30 days	60 days
Expenses (before VAT)	£500	£500

Use the monthly analysis above to calculate creditors. Do not forget to adjust for VAT as necessary.

Note: To simplify this example, it is assumed that purchases change in ratio to usage, ie to sales. In reality, purchases often fluctuate differently from usage for seasonal reasons and creditors at a particular date would depend upon the value of goods *purchased* in the previous month or two, not upon usage.

Value Added Tax

This is not part of the profit and loss account but, as we have seen earlier, it does affect the balance sheet. It is included in the sums owed by customers and to suppliers because it is part of the invoice totals.

There is usually a balance for VAT owing to Customs, which is included in the creditors. It is the net sum of the output tax charged on sales less input tax recovered on purchases.

If a business has only zero-rated sales, there will be a repayment due by Customs since there is no output tax to offset the input tax recoverable. Also, a business which normally pays output tax to Customs could have a repayment due to it for a quarter in which it has exceptionally high input tax on, say, the purchase of a fixed asset.

The VAT balance is not always shown separately. It may be part of the total for creditors, as in the examples of balance sheets earlier in the book. I advise you to put it on its own because it is often a significant amount. Since VAT is payable at the end of the month following the VAT quarter to which it relates, the sum shown in the balance sheet could be due at a time ranging from immediately to three months after the balance sheet date, depending on when the VAT quarter ends. As this is different from when other creditors are due their money, the amount should be shown separately to give a clear view of the financial position of the business.

Calculate the VAT in the example on the following assumptions.

1. The VAT quarter ends on the balance sheet date so the sum outstanding is for the previous three months.
2. The rate is 15 per cent on all sales and purchases.
3. The purchases of materials are the same as usage, though, as explained earlier in the note about creditors, that would not usually be so.
4. The input tax recoverable on overheads was £180 (round this to £200). This may seem low but many of the costs of the business, such as wages, depreciation, rates and insurance are not subject to VAT.

The balance sheet total

Next, calculate the total of the balance sheet under 'represented by', ie capital introduced at the start of the year, which is

£11,000 for both businesses, the value of the fixed assets, plus the profit for the year less drawings of £8,000 for both businesses. The drawings figure is small but both proprietors have had to minimise it in the start-up period. This total is also the figure to fill in above as the proprietor's interest.

Bank overdraft
You calculate this as your last entry on the balance sheet. It is the balancing figure for the balance sheet which makes the figures add up to the proprietor's interest and is proved correct by the source and application of cash statement, as we shall see shortly.

Source and application of cash information

Source of cash
You have calculated the profits. Depreciation is £2,500 for both businesses (not £1,000 – there is £1,500 for vehicles included in the expenses total). There are no sales of fixed assets or loans received.

Application of cash

Payments not chargeable against profits
The only line which applies in this case is owner's drawings.

Changes in working capital
Since this is the first trading year, the figures to be entered are those from the balance sheet at the end of the year. Normally, it would be the changes in the figures from one balance sheet to the other. There are no advance payments by customers in this case.

Cash balances
There were no cash balances at the start of the year. Both businesses have an overdraft which represents the net outflow of cash during the year.

Prudent and Carefree
Source and application of cash for year to 31 December
Year 1

	Prudent £	Carefree £
Source of cash		
Profit for the year before tax		
Add depreciation	_____	_____
Total from trading		
Sale of fixed assets		
Loan received	_____	_____
Total cash available		
Application of cash		
Payments not chargeable against profits		
Fixed assets bought (capital expenditure)		
Owner's drawings	_____	_____
Net cash left in the business	_____	_____
Changes in working capital		
Current assets:		
Stocks (Increase) Decrease		
Debtors (Increase) Decrease		
Payments in advance (Increase) Decrease		
Current liabilities		
Creditors Increase (Decrease)		
VAT payable Increase (Decrease)		
Advance payments		
by customers Increase (Decrease)	_____	_____
Cash (used for) or released from working capital		
Net increase (or decrease) during year in cash held		
Opening bank balance (overdraft)	_____	_____
Closing bank balance (overdraft)	£ _____	£ _____

The closing bank overdraft arrived at here must agree with that calculated on the balance sheet.

Notes on answers to budget exercise – year 1

I now explain how I got to the figures in my answer. Compare yours with mine.

Profit and loss account (answer on page 191)
Did you remember to round to the nearest £100? Rounding is important because it simplifies the figures and saves time both

in writing them down and in adding them up. Better still, rounding makes the results of your efforts easier to understand. Getting rid of unnecessary detail by rounding helps to emphasise the key numbers.

Don't worry about differences of £100 here and there between your figures and my answers. They will probably have occurred because you rounded differently from me. It is whether you remembered the principles and where to put the figures which matters.

How the two businesses compare
The difference in gross profit of 3.6 per cent between the two businesses is the cumulative results of the small variations in the way they control their usage of materials and labour and the discounts for prompt payment obtained by Prudent. At this stage, 3.6 per cent does not sound much. We will see how important it is in a moment. The expenses are the same except for the extra bank interest for Carefree caused by his much higher overdraft – see the balance sheet later.

Prudent and Carefree
Profit and loss account for year to 31 December
Year 1

	Prudent		Carefree	
	%	£	%	£
Sales		100,000		100,000
Materials	25%	25,000	26%	26,000
Cash discounts obtained (2½ % on materials)	(0.6%)	(600)	—	—
Wages	48%	48,000	50%	50,000
Cost of sales	72.4%	72,400	76%	76,000
Gross profit	27.6%	27,600	24%	24,000
Total expenses		12,000		12,000
Bank interest (at 15%)		500		1,200
Depreciation: plant and equipment		1,000		1,000
Net profit	14.1%	£14,100	9.8%	£9,800
Re-stated as				
Proprietor's salary		13,000		13,000
Super profit (loss)		1,100		(3,200)
		£14,100		£9,800

The difference in profitability really shows at super profit level. Those small differences in efficiency mean that Prudent has a small super profit, while Carefree has earned less than a reasonable working wage. Whether you think £13,000 is a reasonable wage depends on who you are and to what extent inflation has affected pay by the time you read this. However, the figure is unimportant. It is the principle which matters. Carefree has earned nothing, no reward at all, for the risk and hassle of running his own business.

Balance Sheet (answer on page 193)

Fixed assets
These are as given in the information with the different depreciation rates applied on cost.

Current assets
Sales are rising rapidly so stocks are based upon the materials' usage for the last two months, *not* on the average for the year. Debtors are similarly based on the last two month's sales. VAT is added to debtors because it is included in sales invoices but not to stocks because it is not part of the cost of stock.

Thus, for stocks, Carefree's figure is £3,100 + £1,850 (half (£3,700) = £4,950 rounded up to £5,000. Carefree's debtors are £12,000 + £14,000 = £26,000 + VAT at 15% = £29,900.

Current liabilities
Creditors are based upon the last two months' usage of materials plus expenses of £500 and include VAT for the same reason as debtors. Thus, for Carefree, the figure is £3,100 + £3,700 + £500 = £7,300 + VAT at 15% = £8,395 rounded to £8,400.

The VAT balance is made up thus:

	Prudent	Carefree
Output tax on sales Oct–Dec	6,000	6,000
Less input tax on materials	1,500	1,560
on overheads	200	200
	£4,300	£4,240

Carefree's input tax is £60 more because his materials usage is £400 greater in the period October to December.

Note also how showing the creditor for VAT separately highlights the fact that this amount is due in 30 days' time. As it is substantial in relation to the other figures, VAT is an important point to take into account in assessing the cash position of many businesses.

The bank overdraft is a balancing figure, as explained earlier. The difference between the two businesses is the cumulative result of better control by Prudent, who has borrowed less than half the amount from the bank that Carefree has.

Prudent and Carefree
Balance sheet as at 31 December
Year 1

	Cost	Accumulated depreciation	Prudent Net book value	Carefree Net book value
Fixed assets	£	£	£	£
Plant and equipment	5,000	1,000	4,000	4,000
Vehicles	6,000	1,500	4,500	4,500
	11,000	2,500	8,500	8,500
Current assets				
Stocks			3,000	5,000
Debtors			21,900	29,900
Payments in advance			500	500
Total current assets			25,400	35,400
Total assets			33,900	43,900
Current liabilities due within one year				
Creditors			4,000	8,400
VAT payable			4,300	4,200
Bank overdraft			8,500	18,500
Total current liabilities			16,800	31,100
Proprietor's interest			£17,100	£12,800
Represented by:				
Capital introduced at start of year			11,000	11,000
Add profit for the year (before tax)			14,100	9,800
			25,100	20,800
Less drawings (actual cash drawn, not notional 'salary')			8,000	8,000
			£17,100	£12,800

Source and application of cash (answer on page 214)
This summarises why, after earning £4,300 less profit than Prudent, Carefree finds his overdraft at £18,500 more than twice that of Prudent.

All the way through Carefree is less efficient than Prudent.

Prudent and Carefree
Source and application of cash for year to 31 December
Year 1

		Prudent £	Carefree £
Source of cash			
Profit for the year before tax		14,100	9,800
Add depreciation		2,500	2,500
Total from trading		16,600	12,300
Sale of fixed assets		—	—
Loan received		—	—
Total cash available		16,600	12,300
Application of cash			
Payments not chargeable against profits			
Fixed assets bought (capital expenditure)		—	—
Owner's drawings		(8,000)	(8,000)
Net cash left in the business		8,600	4,300
Changes in working capital			
Current assets:			
Stocks	(Increase) Decrease	(3,000)	(5,000)
Debtors	(Increase) Decrease	(21,900)	(29,900)
Payments in advance	(Increase) Decrease	(500)	(500)
Current liabilities:			
Creditors	Increase (Decrease)	4,000	8,400
VAT payable	Increase (Decrease)	4,300	4,200
Advance payments by customers	Increase (Decrease)	—	—
Cash (used for) or released from working capital		(17,100)	(22,800)
Net increase or (decrease) during year in cash held		(8,500)	(18,500)
Opening bank balance (overdraft)		—	—
Closing bank balance (overdraft)		£(8,500)	£(18,500)

The differences are not individually decisive but, cumulatively, they are considerable. Carefree is forced by his tight cash situation to take two months' credit from his creditors. Not only does he thereby lose £600 of cash discounts but he is stretching his suppliers' patience. If things go wrong, he has no slack which he can take up. Any more payment delays and he could find credit being refused.

Current ratio
Carefree's current ratio is £35,400/31,100 or 1.1 while Prudent's is £25,400/£16,800 or 1.5.

Acid test
Prudent's debtors cover his current liabilities handsomely while

Carefree's are short by £1,200. If Carefree continues like this he is likely to find his bankers refusing further finance. His creditors will probably become worried at the same time. A *profitable* business will then be in danger of being forced into liquidation by failure to control its cash properly!

Summary
The exercise demonstrates how financial control – or lack of it – can have a dramatic effect upon both the profitability of a company and its ability to stay in business. Carefree is being greedy in his use of cash which is already costing him a substantial part of his profit. Next year it could result in his going out of business. Let's see what happens if we double the figures for next year.

Prudent and Carefree in year 2

This second stage of the exercise supposes that the two businesses double their sales in their second year. I want to show you what happens if Carefree continues to manage his business less well than Prudent.

If you got the figures in year 1 right without much trouble, you may prefer to go straight on to the answers to year 2. If you had difficulty at year 1 or if you would like more practice, I suggest you use the blank forms provided to work the answers out for yourself. The same general points apply as in year 1, the new figures being as follows:

Profit and loss account information

Sales
£200,000 for both businesses.

Materials
Both businesses budget materials at 25 per cent of sales as before, and Carefree again has additional stock wastage, this time of £2,000.

Cash discounts
Prudent continues to obtain 2½ per cent cash discount on his purchases of materials. Round your calculated sum to the nearest £100.

Wages
Both businesses base their contract prices upon 16,000 hours of work at £6 per hour. Carefree works 500 hours of overtime at £8 per hour.

Expenses
These were low in the first year because both owners kept them to a minimum. Although, in year 2, they do not increase in the same ratio as sales, they rise by 50 per cent for Prudent to £18,000. Carefree, as usual, is not so good at controlling his costs so his overheads are £20,000.

Bank interest
£800 for Prudent, £3,600 for Carefree. This time I have assumed that the respective figures of overdraft have decreased or increased at an even rate so the figures are rough calculations based on averages for the overdrafts. Naturally, the interest rate you would use in your own case would be that charged by your bank. As I write this, rates are higher than 15 per cent but they do not usually remain so high for long.

Prudent and Carefree
Profit and loss account for year to 31 December
Year 2

Prudent Last	Carefree Year		Prudent		Carefree	
£	£		%	£	%	£
100,000	100,000	**Sales**				
25,000	26,000	Materials				
(600)	—	Cash discounts obtained				
48,000	50,000	Wages	___		___	
72,400	76,000	Cost of sales	___		___	
27,600	24,000	**Gross profit**				
12,000	12,000	**Total expenses**				
500	1,200	Bank interest (at 15%)				
1,000	1,000	Depreciation: plant and equipment	___		___	
£14,100	£9,800	**Net profit**	%£ ___		%£ ___	
		Re-stated as				
13,000	13,000	Proprietor's salary				
1,100	3,200	Super profit	___		___	
£14,100	£9,800		£ ___		£ ___	

Drawings
£15,000 for each proprietor.

Balance sheet information

Fixed assets
These remain the same, there being no additions during the year. The depreciation rates are unchanged at 20 per cent on original cost (ie the straight-line basis) for plant and equipment and 25 per cent for vehicles.

Prudent and Carefree
Balance sheet as at 31 December
Year 2

Prudent Last	Carefree Year		Cost	Accumulated depreciation	Prudent Net book value	Carefree Net book value
£	£	**Fixed assets**	£	£	£	£
4,000	4,000	Plant and equipment				
4,500	4,500	Vehicles	___	___	___	___
8,500	8,500		___	___	___	___
		Current assets				
3,000	5,000	Stocks				
21,900	29,900	Debtors				
500	500	Payments in advance				
—	—	Cash at bank			___	___
25,400	35,400	Total current assets			___	___
33,900	43,900	Total assets				
		Current liabilities due within one year				
4,000	8,400	Creditors				
4,300	4,200	VAT payable				
8,500	18,500	Bank overdraft			___	___
16,800	31,100	Total current liabilities			___	___
£17,100	£12,800	**Proprietor's interest**			£ ___	£ ___
		Represented by:				
11,000	11,000	Capital at start of year				
14,100	9,800	Add profit for the year (before tax)			___	___
25,100	20,800					
8,000	8,000	Less drawings and tax paid			___	___
£17,100	£12,800				£ ___	£ ___

Current assets and current liabilities

The principles of how you arrive at these figures are the same. Assuming that the sales pattern is similar and that, therefore, the sales and materials usage for the last two months of the second year will be double those of the first year, the balance sheet figures for current assets and current liabilities will also double.

If you wish to work this out for yourself in order to consolidate your understanding, please refer back to the analysis of sales and materials usage given earlier and apply the same calculations to doubled sales. Otherwise, simply double the balance sheet amounts from year 1 which are shown in the last year column on the blank sheets. This applies to all the figures including that for VAT. We will assume, for simplicity, that many of the additional overheads do not carry VAT so the previous amount of £200 included in the total will be about right when doubled as part of the new figure.

Proprietor's interest

This is calculated in the same way as at stage 1 and must be worked out before you arrive at the bank balance.

Bank overdraft

As in year 1, this is calculated as the last entry on the balance sheet, being the figure required to make it balance. If you are working the example, please try this now for Prudent, before reading the next paragraph. If you have trouble with the figure, come back to the text and read on.

Prudent still has a small bank overdraft. Were he to have achieved a credit balance, this would have been shown in current assets, not in current liabilities.

Source and application of cash statement

The same points apply as for year 1, except that last time you filled in the actual figures for the current assets and liabilities because it was the first year of trading. This time you put in the changes up or down on last year.

Comments on the answers at year 2

The same remarks concerning the weaknesses in detailed control by Carefree apply as at year 1. Both businesses have earned

Prudent and Carefree
Source and application of cash for year to 31 December
Year 2

	Prudent £	Carefree £
Source of cash		
Profit for the year before tax		
Add depreciation		
Total from trading	——	——
	——	——
Total cash available		
Application of cash		
Payments not chargeable against profits		
Owner's drawings	——	——
Net cash left in the business	——	——
Changes in working capital		
Current assets:		
Stocks (Increase) Decrease		
Debtors (Increase) Decrease		
Payments in advance (Increase) Decrease		
Current liabilities		
Creditors Increase (Decrease)		
VAT payable Increase (Decrease)	——	——
Cash (used for) or released from working capital		
Net (increase or) decrease during year in overdraft		
Opening bank balance (overdraft)	——	——
Closing bank balance (overdraft)	£___	£___

a profit. That for Carefree may look respectable at first sight but Prudent is now romping away with a figure 50 per cent higher.

Turning to the balance sheet, the difference in the attitudes to the use of cash is shown up more sharply at year 2 than at year 1. While Prudent has managed to reduce his overdraft from £8,500 to £2,700, Carefree has increased his from £18,500 to £30,600. This is not due to any single factor. It is the cumulative result of all those small differences in efficiency.

Referring back to the profit and loss account, you can also see that Prudent is gaining substantially from paying less bank interest. Although this cost has increased, it merely reflects the higher figure at the start of the year. Next year, it will almost disappear whereas, in Carefree's case, it is really beginning to hurt.

As for drawings, though both owners have taken the same sum out of the business, Carefree, as usual, is being more spendthrift. His private expenses are really higher because the total will include a smaller tax bill on the previous year's profit than that paid by Prudent.

Current ratio

Prudent's current ratio at £50,800/£19,300 is now a healthy 2.6 while that for Carefree at £70,800/£55,600 has improved only marginally to 1.3.

Acid test

Prudent's debtors cover his current liabilities even more handsomely than before. Though Carefree's debtors do now cover current liabilities, the margin is tiny in relation to the sums involved.

Prudent and Carefree
Profit and loss account for year to 31 December
Year 2

Prudent Last	Carefree Year		Prudent		Carefree	
£	£		%	£	%	£
100,000	100,000	Sales		200,000		200,000
25,000	26,000	Materials	25%	50,000	26%	52,000
(600)	—	Cash discounts (2½% on materials)	0.6%	(1,200)	—	—
48,000	50,000	Wages	48%	96,000	50%	100,000
72,400	76,000	Cost of sales		144,800		152,000
27,600	24,000	Gross profit	27.6%	55,200	24%	48,000
12,000	12,000	Total expenses		18,000		20,000
500	1,200	Bank interest (at 15%)		800		3,600
1,000	1,000	Depreciation: Plant and equipment		1,000		1,000
£14,100	£9,800	Net profit	18%	£35,400	12%	£23,400
		Re-stated as				
13,000	13,000	Proprietor's salary				
1,100	(3,200)	Super profit				
£14,100	£9,800			£		£

Prudent and Carefree
Balance sheet as at 31 December
Year 2

Prudent Last Year £	Carefree £		Cost £	Accumulated depreciation £	Prudent Net book value £	Carefree Net book value £
		Fixed assets				
		Plant and equip-				
4,000	4,000	ment	5,000	2,000	3,000	3,000
4,500	4,500	Vehicles	6,000	3,000	3,000	3,000
8,500	8,500		11,000	5,000	6,000	6,000
		Current assets				
3,000	5,000	Stocks (Prudent 30 days; Carefree 45 days)			6,000	10,000
21,900	29,900	Debtors (Prudent 45 days; Carefree 60 days)			43,800	59,800
500	500	Payments in advance			1,000	1,000
25,400	35,400	Total current assets			50,800	70,800
33,900	43,900	Total assets			56,800	76,800
		Current liabilities due within one year				
4,000	8,400	Creditors			8,000	16,800
4,300	4,200	VAT payable			8,600	8,400
8,500	18,500	Bank overdraft			2,700	30,400
16,800	31,100	Total current liabilities			19,300	55,600
£17,100	£12,800	Proprietor's interest			£37,500	£21,200
		Represented by:				
11,000	11,000	Capital introduced at start of year			17,100	12,800
14,100	9,800	Add profit for the year (before tax)			35,400	23,400
25,100	20,800				52,500	36,200
8,000	8,000	Less drawings and tax paid			15,000	15,000
£17,100	£12,800				£37,500	£21,200

Moreover, his weaker credit control means that he is much more likely to have bad debts included in his debtors total than Prudent. Since he extends long credit to his customers, they are used to paying slowly and it would not be easy to get the money in quickly, were the bank to ask for a reduction in the overdraft.

Looking at it another way, at the end of year 1, the bank had £18,500 in the business, £5,700 more than the owner's £12,800. Now the figures are £30,400 and £21,200. Given that banks dislike funding a business for a larger sum than the owner, this deficit of £9,200 is looking serious. In contrast, Prudent's bank is now lending him £2,700; compared with his own interest of £37,500, this is minimal.

Prudent and Carefree
Source and application of cash for year to 31 December
Year 2

		Prudent £	Carefree £
Source of cash			
Profit for the year before tax		35,400	23,400
Add depreciation		2,500	2,500
Total from trading		37,900	25,900
Total cash available		37,900	25,900
Application of cash			
Payments not chargeable against profits			
Owner's drawings		15,000	15,000
Net cash left in the business		22,900	10,900
Changes in working capital			
Current assets:			
Stocks	(Increase) Decrease	(3,000)	(5,000)
Debtors	(Increase) Decrease	(21,900)	(29,900)
Payments in advance	(Increase) Decrease	(500)	(500)
Current liabilities:			
Creditors	Increase (Decrease)	4,000	8,400
VAT payable	Increase (Decrease)	4,300	4,200
Cash (used for) or released from working capital		(17,100)	(22,800)
Net (increase) or decrease during year in overdraft		5,800	(11,900)
Opening bank balance (overdraft)		(8,500)	(18,500)
Closing bank balance (overdraft)		£(2,700)	£(30,400)

Does all this really matter?

You may wonder whether this is all as important as I say it is, given that Carefree is making a reasonable profit. Surely the bank won't mind lending him the money to carry on?

Perhaps the bank won't mind. If so, more's the pity! Not all bank managers understand business accounts well enough to spot this kind of situation early enough; many of them continue to lend to a customer like Carefree when it would be in the interests of all concerned if pressure were to be put on him to produce better figures.

As I said in an earlier chapter, businesses may appear to go bust overnight but that is only because the axe has fallen. The trouble probably started a long time (perhaps several years) ago and resulted from the neglect of basic principles.

Compare the two businesses at the end of their second year. Prudent in year 3 will move from an overdraft to money in the bank which he can use to develop the business, start new activities, purchase new equipment etc. Even if the owner doesn't want the business to grow any further, the money in the bank (which has resulted from running it properly) means that, should a recession strike next year, Prudent will be in a much better position to survive a fall in sales than Carefree.

The latter, in mismanaging his business, is running it near the edge of financial disaster. Should anything go wrong, Carefree will have difficulty in putting things right because his problems result from neglecting the details. As I pointed out in the chapters dealing with control of stocks, debtors and creditors, the way a business works cannot be changed overnight. It takes time to achieve financial control.

Alternatively, suppose some new technological development makes it essential for both businesses to re-equip in order to remain competitive. Prudent has cash available and, with a good trading record, he should have no difficulty in borrowing more if he needs to.

If Carefree has to borrow more, he will have to pay substantial interest. The bank or other lenders will ask for security, if they haven't already. Carefree will probably have to look at secondary sources of finance, such as leasing or hire purchase, on which the interest rates are much higher than on bank overdrafts. Carefree is on the slippery slope to ruin!

That was a budget, that was!

Well, that was a budget you have just done! The information I provided you with is what is required to do a simple budget for a small contracting business. The example is not sophisticated; for one thing, the figures ought to be broken down at least by the quarter if not month by month. Nevertheless, even budgeting the annual totals is a start in having a look at the future.

Each of the three statements – profit and loss account, balance sheet and cash flow statement – is an important element. When you start to budget, it is tempting to think that just a profit and loss account will do. The same applies when you begin to produce quarterly or monthly accounts. It takes more work to do the balance sheet as well and you may think that, if the profit looks satisfactory, the balance sheet must be too. After all, it's just a list of the balances resulting from the trading, isn't it? I hope you know the answer to that by now.

Until you have done the balance sheet as well, you have not finished making sense of your figures. There could be a *non sequitur* in your forecast which only becomes apparent once you put the balance sheet together. For instance, you may be expecting a boom year with a marvellous profit but, until you have the balance sheet, you cannot see how much money you will need to finance it. This could be far more than your bank has agreed to lend you or is likely to at the moment.

The balance sheet and source and application of cash statement do not just prove the arithmetic. They show how the money will be used and they may reveal that your plans in their present form cannot be financed.

The decisions needed for a budget

If you look back through the information given, you will see that there are only a few key forecasts or estimates to make in preparing a budget.

The first is sales. The next is the cost of materials. Normally you must estimate this to include wastages because many losses occur without your knowledge. You know they happen but not exactly how or when, so you cannot know their value. I gave you a separate wastage percentage for Carefree as one of the variations in efficiency between the two businesses. In real life, this would simply be a part of the overall difference between the two gross profits.

Those key estimates for sales and gross profit involve by far the biggest figures. Many of the remaining profit and loss ones are of expenses which are individually too small for errors in forecasting them to be important. To simplify the exercise I did not give you the detail of the overheads. In budgeting for a real business, you would have to work them out because it is only by writing down the amounts for each cost that you can make a reasonable assumption as to the overall expenses. Such detail is usually not difficult because few overheads are volatile. Mostly they go up roughly in line with inflation. Some are fixed by contract, like rent. If an overhead alters by more than the inflation rate, it is usually because of some element of your business plan, which you know in advance. Thus, if you plan to hire a salesman and provide him with a car, your motor expenses must rise.

Everything else on the profit and loss account then follows, except for bank interest. This has to be done last, once the balance sheet has been put together because, until you have some idea of the bank overdraft, it is not possible to estimate the interest on it.

Budgeting your balance sheet requires assumptions as to what fixed assets will be required, the amount of credit to be given to customers and how much can be obtained from suppliers. The figures then fall into place.

A little juggling is required between the overdraft and the interest figure. If you balance the balance sheet by putting in an overdraft before allowing for any interest, you will get an idea of the overdraft. Then charging some interest in the profit and loss account increases the overdraft, which again increases the interest! The answer is to round the interest up a bit to allow for this. Like all the other expenses, if you can get it right to within 10 per cent, that will do.

Precise budget figures are not only unimportant; trying to achieve them is a waste of time because fate will change things anyway. If you can get most of the numbers roughly right, you will find that differences between your estimates and the actual costs have a nice habit of tending to cancel each other out so that the overall result is near enough. A rough idea of the future is the best one can hope for but that is sufficient to be a big help in managing the business.

Chapter 21

How Budgeting Will Help ZX Ltd to Put Its House in Order

In the previous chapter we looked at a simple budget for two contracting companies. I showed you how, over a two-year period, the good cash management of Prudent made a big difference to his profits and his ability to succeed; how the bad cash control of Carefree was damaging his profits and putting his future at risk, even though he was still making profits. Bad cash control is insidious. It slowly saps the lifeblood of a business. Good control provides the energy, the cash, needed to develop it.

Now here is a more detailed example. It is for a small manufacturing company this time. In it I will show you how a budget can help you plan to create that energy, to make more profit and to improve your cash flow.

That is what ZX Ltd needs to do. The company is not in a healthy position. Its profits are falling and it is using up cash when it should not be. The example demonstrates how the directors might use a budget to control its finances better and thus manage their way out of trouble.

ZX's figures are tiny but that is deliberate. It is easier to grasp the principles of budgeting with small figures and only a few headings. Once you have understood those principles and the methods illustrated, you will be able to apply them to larger and more complex businesses. Meanwhile, if yours is a larger company, add a nought or two in your mind. If you have several locations, assume that these are the accounts for just one of them. If your list of costs is much longer, it does not matter. Since the principles are the same, extending the list would merely make the example less digestible.

It is now only a few weeks before the end of ZX's financial year on 31 December so it is possible to forecast with some accuracy what the figures will be for the full year. The resulting estimated profit and loss account and balance sheet do not look good. Suppose you have been called in to advise the company on where its financial control is going wrong. What points would you pick up from the figures on pages 208-9? The following background will help you.

This is a small business, whose employees consist of half a dozen workers in its factory and a part-time receptionist/ bookkeeper/typist. The two owner-directors also work in the business. It is unimportant what it makes. Its sales are seasonal, with peaks in the summer and in October and November and a low point in December to February.

ZX is a more complicated business than the ones in my previous examples so the costs are divided under three departments: factory, sales and marketing, and administration. To keep things simple and reduce the amount of information you have to absorb, I have given you the detail for only a few expenses under each heading.

In looking at the figures, concentrate on the key points. There are only a few of these and it does not matter whether the amounts of individual expenses are realistic. Expenses vary from one business to another anyway, and the figures are for the purposes of illustration, rather than indications of what they ought to be. Concentrate on the key figures and ratios, which have been explained in earlier chapters. The profit and loss account and the balance sheet between them will tell you a story about this business, even though you know no more about it than the few facts given you.

Now see what you think that story is before you read my comments.

The problems at ZX Ltd

I hope the first figure you look for in the profit and loss account overleaf is the gross profit ratio since this is the key figure. If you don't make it in gross profit, you can't have it at the net level, so we want to know whether the margin being achieved is right for the kind of business to which the figures relate. ZX is making 40 per cent, a reduction from the 44.1 per cent achieved last year. The fall is bad because, on sales of £370,000, it represents a loss of about £15,000 and accounts for the fall in trading profit of £13,000. However, the position is probably worse because even 44 per cent is too low a gross profit for many manufacturing businesses.

That seems to be so for ZX. I told you nothing about what it makes, though, with only six men and, judging by the balance sheet, a small amount of machinery, it can hardly be in heavy

ZX Ltd
Estimated profit and loss account for the year to
31 December

Last year £		Current year £
340,000	Sales	370,000
24,000	Opening stock	28,000
194,000	Purchases	246,000
(28,000)	Less closing stock	(52,000)
190,000	Cost of sales	222,000
150,000	Gross profit (last year 44.1%) 40%	148,000
52,000	Factory expenses	57,000
24,000	Sales and marketing	25,000
50,000	Administration	52,000
4,000	Cash discounts	4,000
130,000	Total expenses	138,000
5,000	Bank interest	8,000
£15,000	Trading profit	£ 2,000

Note. The costs above include salaries of £12,500 each for the two directors.

industry. As a rough guide, a manufacturer is unlikely to make a respectable profit unless his selling price is at least double his direct manufacturing cost, ie unless he makes at least a 50 per cent gross profit.

This is because his selling and marketing expenses will be high in relation to his sales. No one will buy what he produces unless he gets his sales message across. This usually means calling on prospective buyers either with his own sales force or using agents, together with advertising and promotion in one form or another. Some businesses sell by mail order but have heavy advertising costs instead of salesmen's salaries. In ZX's case, one of the directors handles the selling and the costs are small. Even so, they are important in relation to other expenses.

ZX's 40 per cent gross profit is well short of the target of 50 per cent, so that's the first problem. It could be that its prices are

ZX Ltd
Estimated balance sheet at 31 December of the year just ending

Last year Net book value £		Cost £	Accumulated depreciation £	Current year Net book value £
	Fixed assets			
12,000	Plant and equipment	25,000	18,000	7,000
5,000	Fixtures and fittings	10,000	6,000	4,000
15,000	Vehicles	20,000	10,000	10,000
32,000		55,000	34,000	21,000
	Current assets			
28,000	Stocks			52,000
100,000	Accounts receivable (debtors)			115,000
1,000	Payments in advance			1,000
–	Cash at hand and in bank			–
129,000	**Total current assets**			168,000
161,000	**Total assets**			189,000
	Less			
	Current liabilities due within one year			
55,000	Accounts payable (creditors)			75,000
5,000	VAT payable			6,000
45,000	Bank overdraft			55,000
5,000	Corporation tax payable			1,000
110,000	**Total current liabilities**			137,000
£ 51,000	**Shareholders' interest in the business**			£52,000
	Represented by			
1,000	Share capital			1,000
14,000	Directors' loans			14,000
26,000	Profit and loss account balance at start of year			36,000
10,000	Profit (loss) for the year (after tax)			1,000
£51,000				£52,000

not high enough or that the manufacturing process is inefficient with big wastages of materials or people's time. Probably it is a combination of these weaknesses.

A look at the individual factory, sales and administration expenses confirms this impression because it shows that there is only limited scope for economies. Few of the figures are big enough for a cut of, say 10 per cent, to make much difference.

After wages and salaries, the largest expense is advertising.

An advertising spend of £20,000 is minute in national terms. Many times that amount would be needed for even a small campaign in the national press or on television. This business can only afford to advertise in low cost trade magazines or perhaps in the classified columns of newspapers for mail order. Alternatives are such forms of promotion as stands at trade exhibitions or public relations activity aimed at getting stories into the media about the company. These can be more effective than ordinary advertising.

Whatever the methods used by ZX Ltd, the total of £20,000 is not big enough for there to be obvious scope for reducing it. If ZX is to do any marketing of its products at all, it will have to spend money and 20,000 does not go far. Whether it could be spent more effectively is another matter.

Thus there seems no obvious way to reduce overheads significantly. That is not to say that none of the costs could be cut but trimming overheads is usually not easy. Often the only way to make much of a saving is to stop doing something. That means closing down a department or a location and, usually, making people redundant. I am supposing in my example that there is no scope for that at ZX, which is only a tiny business.

The two directors are taking out only £25,000 between them. At the time I write, the average working wage in the UK is about £9,000, and £12,500 for a boss is too low a reward. It is probably less than the directors could earn working for someone else. Moreover, that is all there is. Only a miserable £1,000 profit after tax is left in the company, so the directors are not restricting their pay in order to build up the business.

Turning to the balance sheet, we find that the directors, who are also the shareholders, have £52,000 in the business. In considering the return they ought to get on this, we should first take into account the interest which could be obtained by selling up and putting the money in a bank or building society. Any interest rate I suggest may be out of date by the time you read this but let us assume the current figure is 10 per cent. Add an extra 10 per cent on top of that as the reward for the risks and responsibility of running one's own business and we have a 20 per cent target for the shareholders' interest in the business. That means a profit of £10,000 after the directors have been paid their salaries. Even that is a small reward for all the extra trouble and the long hours the directors probably work.

Having fallen from last year, the profit is well below that target.

Moreover, £52,000 is not the only money employed in the business because the bank is owed £55,000, up from £45,000 last year. As explained earlier in the book, the return on capital employed should be calculated on the total money used including that lent by the bank. Thus ZX has a total of £107,000 capital employed. Adding back the interest paid to the profit, we have £9,000 – a miserable return. After paying the interest to the bank, there is virtually nothing left to reduce the overdraft or finance expansion.

The reason why the overdraft is high and has risen during the year becomes apparent if we look at the stock and debtor ratios. Comparing the closing stock with the cost of sales for the year is only a crude measure because, as also explained earlier, it is based on averages which are often misleading. However, it is all that can be done unless the monthly figures are available. Here the comparison suggests that the closing stocks represent nearly a quarter of the cost of sales. In other words, there is enough stock to support nearly three months of activity. To be sure that stocks are too high, it would be necessary to compare them with sales for the last two or three months of the trading year or, better still in a seasonal business like this one, with what may be required for *future* sales. Stock is needed to produce the goods expected to be sold in the *next* month or two.

The right level of stocks for ZX Ltd would therefore depend on the anticipated sales for January and February. These are quiet months for this business as they are for many others. This supports the impression gained from the annual figures that stocks are much too high. So does the comparison with last year. Sales have gone up by about 9 per cent from £340,000 to £370,000 but stocks have risen by 86 per cent.

For debtors, we also need to know the monthly sales to assess the position accurately, but grossing up the annual sales to include VAT at 15 per cent offers a rough check. The calculation is £370,000 × 1.15 = £426,000, rounded up to the nearest £1,000. This suggests that debtors at £115,000 are also far too large. They represent well over three months' sales. As we shall see, this business has a sales peak in October and November so the annual average is a little misleading. Still, debtors are up on last year by 15 per cent compared with the 9 per cent sales increase and the company's credit control must leave much to be desired.

Finally, a look at creditors suggests that these are also too high. Grossing up the purchases of £246,000 to include VAT

211

gives an annual figure of £283,000, so more than three months' credit is being taken from suppliers. As with the other ratios, this too should be checked because creditors depend not upon the annual average but upon the goods actually bought in the month or two before the year end. Nevertheless, creditors have risen by 36 per cent (£55,000 to £75,000) compared with 27 per cent for purchases (£194,000 to £246,000). This suggests that more credit is being taken from suppliers. The latter are probably becoming impatient, if not nervous, about their money.

In the above calculation I have not allowed for the fact that the creditors in the balance sheet will include amounts for unpaid expense, not just for purchases of materials. In this business, the expense creditors are only £6,000 and are unlikely to have varied much, so leaving the figure in does not invalidate a crude first appraisal. However, an accurate appreciation of the position would require it to be deducted.

As for the overall solvency of the business, one expects to see a manufacturer's current assets at at least twice his current liabilities because of the stocks he has to hold. The manufacturing process tends to require longer stocking periods than for wholesaling or retailing. Cash flow is often smaller in relation to the money tied up and a greater safety margin is needed.

Here we have a current ratio of 168 ÷ 137 or only 1.2. As for the acid test, debtors at £115,000 are substantially below creditors plus that bank overdraft totalling £130,000. In a manufacturing business the debtors figure often does not cover that for creditors and the overdraft because of the large amounts of working capital needed but, taken with the other figures, this is a further warning sign.

All in all, ZX Ltd appears not to be well run. Let us see how we could forecast the financial results of changing this. For simplicity, I am only giving you a limited amount of information about the business. Before being sure that all the improvements I am about to suggest could be achieved, you would have to check the facts in more detail. If I seem to over-simplify matters, remember that the purpose of this section is to give you an overview of the budgeting process. The more realistic I make this the more complicated it tends to become, so I must take some short cuts and make some assumptions which would not necessarily be true in a real case.

The budget schedules

There are four main budget statements for ZX Ltd: a profit and loss account, a cash flow forecast, a balance sheet, and a source and application of cash statement, together with supporting detailed schedules.

The profit and loss account and cash flow are shown month by month and the large number of figures probably looks intimidating at first, but I will take you through them stage by stage. Glance through them now to see how my budget compares with last year for profits and cash. Don't worry about the detail but a quick overview will help you to make sense of the following. They are on pages 214–16.

General points

Most of the figures on the statements are rounded to the nearest £1,000 and I have eliminated the noughts, ie £18,500 is shown as £18.5. This both simplifies adding up the figures and makes them easier to read. As they may look a little strange, I have left the total columns on the profit and loss and cash flow in full to help you get used to the abbreviated figures.

Budgeted sales

My initial review of the present profit and loss account has suggested that the problem is primarily that more sales are needed and at a better gross profit margin.

I am budgeting to raise sales by 21.6 per cent from £370,000 to £450,000 a year. I have to work out the monthly figures showing how that total will be achieved. Ideally, the estimates should be based on expected sales of each product at the anticipated selling prices. To keep the detail of this example within bounds, I have only prepared the schedule of monthly sales totals on page 215.

This back-up schedule is an important step in any budget because laying the figures out in the right way helps to make them realistic. There is nothing more maddening than getting most of the way through preparing a budget and then spotting a nonsense hidden in a quick estimate. It usually pays to work out the detail from the start. Let us go through the sales schedule column by column.

I start with the month and the number of weeks. I believe in dividing the trading year into periods of five or four weeks

ZX Ltd
Budgeted profit and loss account for the year to 31 December

	Last year £	Budget £	5 Jan £	4 Feb £	4 Mar £	5 Apr £	4 May £	4 Jun £	5 Jul £	4 Aug £	4 Sep £	5 Oct £	4 Nov £	4 Dec £
Sales	370.0	450.0	18.0	22.0	26.0	60.0	40.0	36.0	30.0	28.0	28.0	60.0	80.0	22.0
Opening stock	28.0	52.0	52.0	50.2	48.0	62.4	48.2	42.4	38.9	34.3	49.7	73.2	57.0	28.4
Purchases	246.0	222.0	9.0	11.0	30.0	20.0	17.0	17.0	11.0	30.0	38.0	15.0	13.0	11.0
Less closing stock	(52.0)	(28.0)	(50.2)	(48.0)	(62.4)	(48.2)	(42.4)	(38.9)	(34.3)	(49.7)	(73.2)	(57.0)	(28.4)	(28.0)
Cost of sales	222.0	246.0	10.8	13.2	15.6	34.2	22.8	20.5	15.6	14.6	14.5	31.2	41.6	11.4
40% Gross profit 45.3%	148.0	204.0	7.2	8.8	10.4	25.8	17.2	15.5	14.4	13.4	13.5	28.8	38.4	10.6
Factory expenses	57.0	71.0												
Sales and marketing	25.0	35.0												
Administration	52.0	64.0												
Cash discounts	4.0	5.0												
Total expenses	138.0	175.0												
Bank interest	8.0	6.5												
Trading profit	2.0	22.5												
Profit on sale of fixed assets	-	1.0												
Net profit	£ 2.0	£23.5												

Remaining analysis not done at this stage.

214

Gross sales schedule

Month and no of weeks	Sales/week	Sales net	VAT on sales	Sales gross
	£	£	£	£
Jan 5	3.6	18.0	2.7	20.7
Feb 4	5.5	22.0	3.3	25.3
Mar 4	6.5	26.0	4.0	30.0
			10.0	
Apr 5	12.0	60.0	9.0	69.0
May 4	10.0	40.0	6.0	46.0
Jun 4	9.0	36.0	5.4	41.4
			20.4	
Jul 5	6.0	30.0	4.5	34.5
Aug 4	7.0	28.0	4.1	32.1
Sep 4	7.0	28.0	4.2	32.2
			12.8	
Oct 5	12.0	60.0	9.0	69.0
Nov 4	20.0	80.0	12.0	92.0
Dec 4	3 at 7.3	22.0	3.3	25.3
			24.3	
Total		£450.0	£67.5	£517.5

Gross purchases schedule

Purchases net	VAT on purchases	Purchases gross	Opening creditors Add	Closing creditors Deduct	Payments
£	£	£	£	£	£
9.0	1.3	10.3	69.0	42.3	37.0
11.0	1.7	12.7	42.3	29.7	25.3
30.0	4.5	34.5	29.7	49.2	15.0
	7.5				
20.0	3.0	23.0	49.2	55.2	17.0
17.0	2.5	19.5	55.2	38.7	36.0
17.0	2.6	19.6	38.7	34.3	24.0
	8.1				
11.0	1.7	12.7	34.3	26.0	21.0
30.0	4.5	34.5	26.0	47.0	13.5
38.0	5.7	43.7	47.0	60.0	30.7
	11.9				
15.0	2.2	17.2	60.0	39.0	38.2
13.0	2.0	15.0	39.0	25.0	29.0
11.0	1.6	12.6	25.0	20.0	17.6
	5.8				
£222.0	£33.3	£255.3			£304.3

VAT quarterly payments schedule

		Output tax	Purchases	Input tax	Net payable	Payments
Jan–Mar	Sales	10.0		7.5		
	Assets sold	.5	Assets bought	1.5		
		10.5		9.0	1.5	6.0
Apr–Jun	Sales	20.4	Purchases	8.1	12.3	1.5
Jun–Sep	Sales	12.8	Purchases	11.9	.9	12.3
Oct–Dec	Sales	24.3	Purchases	5.8	18.5	.9
	Total				33.2	20.7

216

rather than into calendar months. The number of selling days varies from one calendar month to another. Take April. If a manufacturer does not despatch on a Saturday, he has five selling days per week. If Easter is in April and he does not work on Good Friday or the following bank holiday Monday, he may have only 18 selling days in the month, depending on when the weekends fall, compared with 20 in February. Yet this is nominally two days shorter than April. Working in calendar months creates artificial distortions which make it difficult to compare one month with another or with past years.

If you budget in periods of four or five weeks, at least you know that each period is comparable, subject only to holidays.

The second column shows sales per week. It is better to start the estimates from sales per week rather than from totals per period because it is easier to make allowances for, say, Christmas week. For a retailer that week may be very busy but, for a manufacturer, it may be dead. In December, I have planned for only three weeks at £7,300 per week. I have assumed that no orders are received in the fourth week containing the Christmas holiday.

Planning in sales per week takes care of the difference between four- and five-week periods and also helps to make sure that the budgeted sales show a logical progression from peak to trough.

Having estimated the sales per week, it is easy to calculate the total per period. Calling the periods January, February etc, even though they do not correspond precisely, is no problem because they all start and stop at a weekend and one soon gets used to the fact that this is not always at the calendar month end.

The next columns calculate the VAT on the sales and the gross sales including VAT. I will need to know the output VAT on the sales each quarter and the gross sales figures period by period later for the cash flow.

The next set of columns deals with purchases. I will come back to those later.

Once I had broken the sales budget down into 12 periods, I entered the annual and period figures in the appropriate columns of the profit and loss budget.

The gross profit calculation
The next figure to be decided is the gross profit percentage. Since the ratio is unsatisfactory at only 40 per cent, I must

decide what can be achieved next year. My target is 50 per cent but I know that this will not be achieved at once. Improvements in manufacturing efficiency may only come gradually. I have therefore assumed that the business will achieve only the existing 40 per cent for the first three months. In the next three months, I hope for an improvement to 43 per cent and in the last six months to 48 per cent. This will allow time to put things right.

Estimating the figures period by period to produce a calculated annual result of 45.3 per cent gives me a logical basis for the overall result and also produces a more realistic budget. If I were to take the short cut of making an overall estimate, first I would be unlikely to guess accurately the average resulting from a progressive improvement to 50 per cent; second, using an average would create shortfalls on budget in the first three months and gains towards the end of the year, which would be meaningless.

The cost of sales calculation

Now that I have a figure for sales and another for gross profit, I can calculate the cost of sales as the difference between the two. I already know the opening stock which leaves just the purchases and the closing stock to calculate.

The easiest way of doing this is to work out a target for the stock at the end of the year. This is done by looking at what will be needed as goods to be sold in January and February for the year following the budget year. I can see that the cost of sales for January and February this year will be £24,000. Assuming that sales continue to improve in the following year, I estimate the stock at 31 December at £28,000 to cover the following two months' sales.

This is a guesstimate, but it has a logical basis. It is only just over half the present stock level but the business has far too much money tied up in stock at present. It may be optimistic to suppose that I can reduce the stock by as much as this while increasing sales but that is the target. I may need to adjust it later when I can see the whole picture of the budget and learn more about the business, but it will do for the time being.

Now I can work out the total purchases for the year because that is the balancing figure; ie my cost of sales, £246,000, will be found partly from the stock reduction of £24,000 so I deduct that sum to give the purchases required – £222,000.

The next step is to work out the detailed purchases and stock, period by period: purchases first. Both fluctuate during the year as materials are bought to manufacture the stock needed to meet the sales targets. Rather than try to forecast the stock figures, it is simpler to estimate purchase figures month by month. In doing so, I allow for the effects of the planned action to reduce the stock levels which means that part of the cost of sales will be met from existing stocks rather than from fresh purchases.

The timing of purchases must allow for buying in ahead of the sales peaks. You can see that these are in April to June and October and November. I plan for purchases to peak a month earlier in the first case and two months earlier at the end of the year. I allow two months then because the sales figures are bigger and because the factory will want to spread the production over a longer period, rather than work flat out immediately before the goods have to be despatched. The production system is probably not flexible enough for that, anyway.

Inaccuracies in the forecast timing of purchases of goods do not affect the budgeted profit but they do have an impact on cash flow. As they are an important element of this, a realistic forecast is important.

Now I can work out the stock at the end of each period. I know the starting figure in January, together with the expected purchases and cost of sales, so I calculate the closing stock. That then becomes the opening stock for February and I repeat the calculations period by period through to December to arrive at the same closing stock, £28,000, which I estimated earlier. If this does not work when you try it for your own business, there is an error in your arithmetic.

Budgeting for the expenses
On page 220 you will find my budget of the expenses for the factory, for sales and marketing, and for administration. I began by putting down totals only. I did not worry about detail at this stage because I wanted a look at the end result first – the profit and the bank balance.

When you budget, I suggest you do the same. There is no point in working out the expenses period by period only to find an unsatisfactory end result. The sales or the gross profit figures may have to be revised to produce a more satisfactory answer. One wants to be sure the annual totals produce acceptable profit and cash figures before tackling the detailed analysis. I budgeted for a 25 per cent increase in the factory pay rates to

ZX Ltd
Expenses budget for the year to 31 December

Last year £		Total year £	
	Factory		
40.0	Production wages	50.0	*Monthly analysis not*
2.0	Electricity	3.0	*done at this stage.*
3.0	Repairs	4.0	
7.0	Sundries	8.0	
52.0		65.0	
5.0	Depreciation on plant and equipment	6.0	
£57.0		£71.0	
	Sales and marketing		
20.0	Advertising	27.0	
2.0	Sales brochures	3.0	
3.0	Sundries	5.0	
£25.0		£35.0	
	Administration		
5.0	Salaries: Staff	10.0)	
25.0	Directors	28.0)	
5.0	Motor	6.0)	
4.0	Rent	4.0)	
1.7	Rates	2.0)	
0.8	Telephone	1.0)	
0.5	Insurance	0.5)	
1.0	Professional fees	1.5)	
3.0	Sundries	5.0)	
£46.0	Subtotal	£58.0	
	Depreciation,		
1.0	Fixtures and fittings	1.0)	
5.0	Vehicles	5.0)	
£52.0	Total administration	£64.0	

allow either for increased overtime or extra staff, who would be needed to produce the higher production required to meet the sales forecast.

To budget for wages properly, list the names of employees and their current wages, allowances etc, and then estimate what increases they will each be given and when. I have done only a simplified guess.

The short cut I took here is dangerous when preparing a budget because wages are usually one of the largest expenses. The precise amount of a pay increase and when it will be paid often have a significant effect on the figures. Moreover, listing the people employed by department helps to ensure that staff increases or reductions are allowed for. For instance, it would be foolish to budget for a doubled sales figure without considering whether any more people were required to produce the extra goods. I also allowed for more staff in administration, which includes the accounting. The present figure suggests that only a part-time clerk is employed and I allowed for an increase to provide the resources needed to make the planned improvements in credit and stock control.

Most of the planned increases in the rest of the figures are about 10 per cent, including the directors' salaries. The exception is the advertising expenditure. To take account of the planned 20 per cent increase in sales, I put this up from £20,000 to £27,000 because the extra sales will not just happen. They will have to be achieved by extra marketing effort, which is likely to cost more.

As I explained in my opening comments on the current year figures, the expenses shown are typical of those found under the various headings, but they are only examples. In many businesses, there would be sales and marketing staff so a wages figure would appear under that heading as well as for the factory and for administration.

Cash discounts to customers
This is the next figure to work out. Sometimes it is shown as a deduction from sales. I believe in showing it as an expense because it is really a kind of interest charge. It relates to the financial policy of the business rather than being a cost of sales.

One can estimate what cash discounts will have to be given to customers on the basis of the figure for last year and I have used the same percentage rounded up to the nearest £1,000. Though persuading customers to pay more promptly may mean some increase in cash discounts, this will probably not be much because the high value of debtors is likely to be a result of allowing them credit beyond the normal terms. Getting them to pay on time will not necessarily mean that more of them take the cash discount.

Some businesses offer a discount for payment within seven days, others at 30 days. In the section on credit control I explain how expensive it is to give discounts. To encourage its debtors to pay up more quickly, the ZX Company will rely on proper credit control procedures including prompt rendering of invoices and timely chasing-up of slow payers rather than the costly inducement of cash discounts.

Now I can add up the total expenses column.

Interest payable

The loans from the directors are interest free so the interest paid is on the overdraft. At this stage, I do not know what the overdraft will be at the end of December next year, let alone how it will vary during the year, so I can only make a guess that I may be able to reduce it sufficiently for interest next year to come down from £8,000 to, say, £5,000. That's not the figure you can see in the profit and loss account because I had to amend it later, as I will explain.

The trading profit

I can now calculate a budgeted trading profit of £24,000 (£22,500 plus the preliminary underestimate of interest, £1,500). That seems satisfactory since it will allow for an increase in the directors' salaries to a more realistic level and provide some 'super profit' as a return on the capital invested. We saw earlier that there is no such super profit at present.

The next figure is a profit on the sale of fixed assets. Often, it is not known whether a profit or loss will be made on the sale of fixed assets during the year and it is usually unimportant anyway. I put in a figure here because I know that ZX is likely to sell an old machine for £3,000 plus VAT. Its net book value, ie the figure written down by depreciation, is only £2,000, so there will be a surplus of £1,000.

Now I need to see what overdraft will result from these figures by the end of next year. The profit may be satisfactory but what about the cash position? I put aside the profit and loss budget

ZX Ltd
Cash flow forecast for the year to 31 December

	£	
Opening debtors	115,000	
Add credit sales including VAT	517,500	*As text explains*
Less closing debtors	(71,000)	*analysis not*
discounts allowed	(5,000)	*done at this*
		stage.
Cash in from debtors	556,500	
Cash sales including VAT	–	
Assets sold	3,500	
Total cash in	560,000	
Goods including VAT	304,300	

Expenses including VAT

Monthly

Salaries and wages	88,000
Advertising	27,000
Factory	12,000
Sales and marketing	8,000
Administration	11,000

Quarterly

Rent	4,000
Electricity	3,000
Telephone	1,000
Professional fees	1,500
VAT	20,700
Bank charges and interest	6,500

Six monthly

Rates	2,000

Annual

Insurance	500
Total expenses	185,200
Capital expenditure	11,500
Tax paid	1,000
Total cash out	502,000
Net cash flow	58,000
Opening bank balance	(55,000)
Closing bank balance	**£3,000**

for the time being, without analysing the expenses period by period, and start on the cash flow forecast.

The cashflow forecast (page 223)
I start the cash flow forecast by putting in the gross figures for sales including VAT, which I worked out earlier on the sales schedule. I use the gross figures because these are the amounts which the customers will pay to the company. The cash flow forecast shows how money will flow in and out of the company, so the sums are not the same as those in the profit and loss account. The VAT included will have to be passed on to the government and this is shown later as a payment.

In the total column I fill in the opening debtors, this being the figure from the estimated balance sheet drawn up as at the end of the current year. Then I work out the closing debtors by making an assumption as to how much credit ZX Ltd will allow customers by the end of next year. I assume this to be six weeks' sales, which means the whole of the gross sales for the December four-week period plus half the previous one in November, ie £25,300 plus £46,000, which I round down to £71,000.

The discounts allowed I already know to be £5,000, as in the profit and loss account. At this stage, I do not work all the figures out period by period. I first want to do the total column to see what the overdraft will look like at the end of the year.

Now I can calculate the total cash expected to be received from debtors, this being the opening debtors plus the sales on credit, less the closing debtors and discounts allowed.

The next line is for cash sales. Many manufacturers have cash sales in a factory shop or from sales to staff, in the canteen etc. ZX Ltd does not, but I put the line in to show you where such sales would go.

Next come sales of fixed assets. As already mentioned, a machine is to be sold for £3,000 plus VAT, which I round to £3,500. Now I calculate the total of cash coming in at £560,000.

Payments for goods including VAT
No cash flow forecast is useful unless you can make a sensible estimate of how much will have to be paid to the suppliers of goods and materials and when. These payments usually dwarf all others, except perhaps wages and salaries. Fortunately, the task is not as difficult as it sounds. Payments to suppliers derive logically from the purchases period by period, which have

already been worked out for the profit and loss budget.

Look at the purchase payments schedule, which is alongside the sales schedule on page 215. First, I listed the purchases from the profit and loss budget. These values for goods received do not include VAT. To arrive at the totals invoiced by suppliers, I added VAT to give the gross figures. It was convenient to note the VAT amounts for sales only earlier, because later I needed both the output and input tax figures to calculate the quarterly VAT payments.

To estimate the actual payments by period to suppliers, I have to allow for changes in the total owing to creditors. At the start of the budget year, this is £69,000. The difference of £6,000 between this and the £75,000 shown in the balance sheet is the expense creditors, which relate to overheads, not purchases.

To arrive at the creditors at the end of each period, I assume that the period of credit obtained by ZX Ltd from its suppliers will be gradually reduced. By the end of the year, I expect it to be down to about six weeks, ie the purchases including VAT for December, £12,600 plus half those for November, £7,500, or £20,100, rounded down to £20,000.

In planning to cut the credit taken from suppliers to as little as six weeks, I may have been pessimistic about the amount of credit which can be obtained. Many businesses do not pay as promptly, especially in manufacturing. However, your creditors are someone else's debtors and, just as I was planning to get the debtors down to six weeks, so may the suppliers to ZX Ltd be planning the same thing. Given that the company was taking extended credit and that, as a result, some of its suppliers were probably unhappy, I assume that there will be pressure for more prompt payment and that it is wise to improve relationships with suppliers by paying on time. Moreover, this may enable better buying terms or prompt payment discounts to be negotiated.

Once I have estimated the closing creditors, I can work out the total payments of £304,300. For the moment, I leave the analysis period by period. I only need the total payments at this stage.

Staff costs

I like to show all the staff costs together as one total in a cash flow forecast because this makes it easy to compare the actual payments with the budget for each period. Whatever your wages system, you will know the total wages and salaries paid each week or month for the entire company. If the corresponding budget figure is in the cash flow forecast, it is easy to compare actual with budget. This is important as it is one of the largest expenses in many businesses. Often the same figure in the profit and loss account is broken down over several departments, so it is useful to have the total in the cash flow forecast.

The expense payments for the cash flow forecast
Theoretically, you should consider whether there is likely to be any increase in the expenses outstanding at the end of the year. In practice the expense creditors often do not change enough to matter since the same costs, such as electricity and telephone, tend to be outstanding each time.

It is not worth worrying about small increases in the creditors for individual expenses. If you know there is a large item, such as advertising, for which the amount unpaid at the end of the year is bigger than last time, increase the closing creditor and reduce the payment forecast for it. Otherwise, assume that the payments will be the sums as budgeted in the profit and loss account. Minor variations in expense creditors do not matter.

I do not think it is worthwhile calculating the VAT on expenses either. The profit and loss budget figures are net while the payments will be gross but there will be a compensating reduction in the VAT payments. One can spend a lot of time working out how much input tax there is on expenses only to find that it is too small to matter.

I therefore put in the totals of the expenses from the profit and loss account, *except for depreciation*.

As depreciation is not a cash payment, it is not part of the cash flow forecast. That is why I show depreciation at the bottom of the analysis of expenses so that the totals of all the cash items can be conveniently calculated for the cash flow forecast and the ones including depreciation used for the profit and loss account.

Although I use the same expense totals, you will see that I break them down between monthly, quarterly, six monthly and annual. At this stage I still do not spread them across the periods but, in due course, take into account that some items will be paid quarterly or less frequently, although an estimated amount is included in the profit and loss account for each period.

The VAT payments

Though Value Added Tax is not an expense for profit and loss purposes, it is an important part of cash flow.

On the schedule of sales and purchase payments on page 215, I calculated the VAT quarterly payments by deducting from the VAT totals added to sales those for purchases. I adjusted for the output tax on the fixed asset sale and for the input tax on the replacement to be bought. I ignored input tax on expenses to keep things simple.

The creditor in the balance sheet at the start of the year will be the first quarterly payment, whereas the outstanding VAT for the last quarter will be a corresponding creditor in the balance sheet. The latter increases from £6,000 to £18,500. The rise of £12,500 accounts for the difference between the VAT payable, £33,200, and that actually paid, £20,700.

Now I add the total expenses on the cash flow, £183,700.

I put in the capital expenditure – a machine to be bought in February for £10,000 plus VAT.

The bank interest figure I enter is the provisional one of £5,000 used earlier in the profit and loss account. Later it will be raised to £6,500.

There will be a tax payment of £1,000 at the end of the year relating to the previous year. As these are single figures, I put them in in the appropriate periods at the same time as in the total column but I have still not calculated all the period figures for the rest of the items. Now I add up the total outgoings – £500,500.

Closing bank overdraft

I can now see what the overdraft will be. I have a figure for total cash in, £560,000, less total outgoings, £500,500, which gives me a net cash flow of £59,500. Putting in the opening bank balance, £55,000, which, being an overdraft, is in brackets, shows that, at the end of the year, ZX Ltd will have £4,500 in the bank (subsequently adjusted to £3,000).

This looks satisfactory so I can move on to the details period by period. I do this for the cash flow forecast first rather than for the profit and loss account, because I want to see the period

227

overdrafts. Then I will be able to work out the bank interest more accurately.

Completing the cash flow forecast period by period
The sales figures including VAT for each period come from the sales schedule. I spread the cash discounts by using the same percentage for each period as for the whole year. That calculation is not accurate for 30-day discounts because many of them will be given in the following period, but the figures here are too small for this to matter.

Now I can work out the closing debtors for each period. I start in January in the same way as I arrived at the stocks in the profit and loss account, ie the opening debtors at the beginning of January are the same as from the total column, £115,000. To that I add the sales of £20,700 and deduct discounts allowed, £200. I then estimate the closing debtors assuming that, initially, the same extended credit will be allowed to customers. The basis is thus the sales figures for the last two periods of the current year plus the budget figure for January. The current year sales figures are not quoted. You will obtain them from your current records.

I now have the opening debtors for February and I repeat the process, gradually reducing the number of weeks' credit allowed to customers during the year. The *total* of debtors does not reduce steadily because, when the sales rise at the two peak periods, so do the debtors. Nevertheless, reducing the length of credit allowed means that, by the end of the year, I am back to my forecast figure of £71,000.

Having worked out the debtors at the end of each period, I can fill in the lines for cash received from debtors and total cash in.

For the next line, payments to suppliers for materials in each period, I go back to the analysis of purchases. There I fill in the closing creditors period by period, reducing in stages the number of weeks' credit taken from suppliers, just as I based the debtors on shorter credit periods allowed to them. This gives me the period payments.

Spreading the expenses in the cash flow forecast
In this budget, I make the staff costs similar for each period. A more detailed budget will show an increase in the period in which a pay rise is to be granted or extra staff taken on.

I round the figures to the nearest £100 and, in order to do so, have to have some periods at £6.8k and others at £7.0k. Such minor distortions do not matter since the period profit does not mean a great deal anyway, as I will explain later. Moreover, rounding variations in other figures tends to iron out such differences.

The advertising spend is not going to be the same each period and I allow for expected peaks and troughs.

Next I analyse the rest of the expenses according to whether they are monthly, quarterly, six monthly or annual. All the monthly expenses for the factory, sales and marketing, and administration headings can be added up and spread as a single total which is quick, simple and avoids fiddling about with tiny monthly sums. Having one period total also irons out the inevitable minor distortions owing to irregular payment of bills and makes it easier to see the overall picture when comparing the budget with the actual results later, period by period.

Although I separate the quarterly and monthly expenses, it may not be necessary to do so in your business. As my example shows, the quarterly payments tend to fall in different periods so that, overall, there is not much difference between an accurate spread of the payments and one arrived at by averaging. Are any of your quarterly paid expenses large enough to make it worthwhile calculating the spread accurately, or is any likely distortion so small that you can save time by including them in the period total to be divided by 12?

Now I am able to work out the total expenses and the total cash out lines period by period. After that comes the net cash flow period by period. This is the difference between the lines for total cash in and total cash out.

The bank overdraft period by period
I then calculate the closing bank overdrafts for each period. The starting figure in January is the same as that in the total column. Each closing figure becomes the starting one for the next period and you should arrive in December at the same calculated balance. If you cannot get back to the same closing figure in your final period as you already have in the total column, there is something wrong with your arithmetic. At this stage, my figure is £4,500 because I am still using my first estimate for bank interest.

An important point about the overdraft
I now see that, though there will be cash in the bank at the end

ZX Ltd

Cash flow forecast for the year to 31st December

	Total year £	5 Jan £	4 Feb £	4 Mar £	5 Apr £	4 May £	4 Jun £	5 Jul £	4 Aug £	4 Sep £	5 Oct £	4 Nov £	4 Dec £
Opening debtors	115,000	115.0	105.5	89.6	73.3	102.6	115.1	85.1	72.3	60.1	55.0	90.3	129.4
Add credit sales including VAT	517,000	20.7	25.3	30.0	69.0	46.0	41.4	34.5	32.1	32.2	69.0	92.0	25.3
Less closing debtors	(71,000)	(105.5)	(89.6)	(73.3)	(102.6)	(115.1)	(85.1)	(72.3)	(60.1)	(55.0)	(90.3)	(129.4)	(71.0)
discounts allowed	(5,000)	(.2)	(.2)	(.3)	(.7)	(.5)	(.4)	(.3)	(.3)	(.3)	(.7)	(.9)	(.2)
Cash in from debtors	556,500	30.0	41.0	46.0	39.0	33.0	71.0	47.0	44.0	37.0	33.0	52.0	83.5
Cash sales including VAT	—												
Assets sold	3,500			3.5									
Total cash in	560,000	30.0	41.0	49.5	39.0	33.0	71.0	47.0	44.0	44.0	37.0	52.0	52.0
Goods including VAT	304,300	37.0	25.3	15.0	17.0	36.0	24.0	21.0	13.5	30.7	38.2	29.0	17.6
Expenses including VAT													
Monthly													
Salaries and wages	88,000	7.3	7.4	7.3	7.4	7.3	7.4	7.3	7.4	7.3	7.3	7.3	7.3
Advertising	27,000		1.0	2.0	4.0	2.0	2.0	2.0	1.0	1.0	4.0	4.0	4.0
Factory	12,000												
Sales and marketing	8,000												
Administration	16,000	2.5	2.6	2.6	2.6	2.6	2.6	2.5	2.6	2.6	2.6	2.6	2.6

Quarterly												
Rent	4,000			1.0			1.0			1.0			1.0
Electricity	3,000			1.0			.5			1.0			.5
Telephone	1,000			.2			.3			.2			.3
Professional fees	1,500			.3			.2						.8
VAT	20,700	6.0			1.5		.7	12.3			.9		
Bank charges and interest	6,500			2.5			2.0			1.0			1.0
Six monthly												
Rates	2,000						1.0						1.0
Annual												
Insurance	500					.5							
Total expenses	185,200	16.3	11.2	16.4	15.5	12.2	17.2	24.1	11.2	13.4	14.8	14.2	18.7
Capital expenditure	11,500		11.5										
Tax paid	1,000						1.0						
Total cash out	502,000	53.3	48.0	31.4	32.5	48.2	41.2	45.1	24.7	44.1	53.0	44.2	36.3
Net cash flow	58,000	(23.3)	(7.0)	18.1	6.5	(15.2)	29.8	1.9	19.3	(7.1)	(20.0)	7.8	47.2
Opening bank balance	(55,000)	(55.0)	(78.3)	(85.3)	(67.2)	(60.7)	(75.9)	(46.1)	(44.2)	(24.9)	(32.0)	(52.0)	(44.2)
Closing bank balance	£3,000	(78.3)	(85.3)	(67.2)	(60.7)	(75.9)	(46.1)	(44.2)	(24.9)	(32.0)	(52.0)	(44.2)	3.0

of the year, the overdraft will peak at £85,300 at the end of February and will not be below its starting figure of £55,000 until the end of June, halfway through the year. That cash balance of £4,500, looked at in isolation, is misleading. The business will have only just gone into credit at the bank and, at the end of October, it will still have an overdraft of £51,900.

The bank interest recalculated

I can arrive at a more accurate figure for bank interest. I could have calculated it period by period but, since the figure was not large enough to be a key factor in the cash flow, I worked out a rough average for each quarter. My quick and crude estimates may have overstated the likely interest but the rate could rise and it is better to be cautious.

Increasing the interest from £5,000 to £6,500, the total of my four quarterly calculations, now alters the period totals and reduces the final bank balance to £3,000.

The profit and loss budget period by period

I now return to the profit and loss budget. The increased interest reduces the trading profit to £22,500. The figures can be filled in period by period because I know that the budgeted profit and the cash flow for the year are satisfactory. I explained earlier that I had avoided analysing them period by period until now because I only needed the total for the year at first. Any fine tuning of the annual totals – such as for interest – would affect the period analysis and this was therefore best left until last.

The annual totals of the factory, sales and marketing, and administration expenses, shown on pages 234–5 have to be spread by period. The factory wages and the administration salaries add up to the total for the whole company shown in the cash flow and are subtotals from the wages schedule.

I next total and average the rest of the expenses as a single figure each period. The period totals are then filled in on the profit and loss budget on page 236.

The cash discounts come from the cash flow forecast.

I spread the bank overdraft interest equally, some periods being rounded to £500, others to £600. An alternative is to enter the expected amounts in the periods in which they will have to be paid. Indeed, some accountants suggest doing this for the quarterly, six monthly and annual expenses, such as electricity, telephone, rates and insurance, in the profit and loss budget, just as I have in the cash flow. They argue that it simplifies the arithmetic and allows you to compare the budgeted payment with the actual payment, instead of using monthly averages to build up provisions until the actual bills come in.

I do not think there is one right way. Both methods have advantages. I prefer to spread the figures equally because non-accountants tend to look at the trading profit or loss each period as an indicator of the results for that period.

The real meaning of the trading profit analysis period by period
This leads on to the next point. Will the business really make a loss in seven of the 12 periods? My figures suggest losses in January, February, March, July, August, September and December. Do they mean that ZX Ltd will trade unprofitably for over half the year?

If the expenses are averaged as I have done, it is true that ZX Ltd will make an arithmetical or notional loss in those periods, but this is only a bookkeeping figure. What matters is that, overall, there will be a profit. The business cannot trade for some periods of the year only. It has to operate for the entire 12 months and, in some of those which are apparently unprofitable, it will be building up stock ready to sell in the peak periods.

You must not judge any one period in isolation. All that the period figures do is to provide a means by which to measure results and progress during the year. What matters is whether you have made a bigger or a smaller profit (or loss) than you forecast at each stage. That comparison shows how you are doing the year in comparison with the plan.

If the amounts of the expenses are not averaged but budgeted for in the periods in which they will be paid, this accentuates some of the differences from one period to another. Some differences cancel out since some quarterly bills fall in one period, some in another. Nevertheless, I feel that non-accountants are more likely to misinterpret a statement produced that way.

When looking at how the business performs in each period, it may be more helpful to consider the gross profit line. This shows the contribution earned towards the overheads of the business. In my example, the amount varies widely. One of ZX Ltd's problems is that it has peaks and troughs in its trading and, during the troughs, it does not earn enough gross profit to pay its fixed expenses. This highlights the possibilities of

ZX Ltd
Budget for the year to 31 December

Last year £		Total year £	Jan £	Feb £	Mar £	Apr £	May £	June £	July £	Aug £	Sept £	Oct £	Nov £	Dec £
	Factory													
40.0	Production wages	50.0	4.1	4.2	4.1	4.2	4.1	4.2	4.1	4.2	4.2	4.2	4.2	4.2
2.0	Electricity	3.0 ⎫												
3.0	Repairs	4.0 ⎬	1.3	1.2	1.3	1.2	1.3	1.2	1.3	1.2	1.3	1.2	1.3	1.2
7.0	Sundries	8.0 ⎭												
52.0		65.0	5.4	5.4	5.4	5.4	5.4	5.4	5.4	5.4	5.5	5.4	5.5	5.4
5.0	Depreciation on plant	6.0	.5	.5	.5	.5	.5	.5	.5	.5	.5	.5	.5	.5
£57.0		£71.0	5.9	5.9	5.9	5.9	5.9	5.9	5.9	5.9	6.0	5.9	6.0	5.9
	Sales and marketing													
20.0	Advertising	27.0	—	1.0	2.0	4.0	2.0	2.0	2.0	1.0	1.0	4.0	4.0	4.0
2.0	Sales brochures	3.0 ⎫	.6	.7	.6	.7	.6	.7	.6	.7	.7	.7	.7	.7
3.0	Sundries	5.0 ⎭												
£25.0		£35.0	.6	1.7	2.6	4.7	2.6	2.7	2.6	1.7	1.7	4.7	4.7	4.7

Administration

Salaries: Staff	5.0	10.0												
Directors	25.0	28.0	3.2	3.1	3.2	3.1	3.2	3.1	3.2	3.1	3.2	3.2	3.2	3.2
Motor	5.0	6.0												
Rent	4.0	4.0												
Rates	1.7	2.0												
Telephone	0.8	1.0												
Insurance	0.5	0.5												
Professional fees	1.0	1.5	1.7	1.6	1.7	1.6	1.7	1.6	1.7	1.6	1.7	1.7	1.7	1.7
Sundries	3.0	5.0												
Subtotal	£46.0	£58.0	4.9	4.7	4.9	4.7	4.9	4.7	4.9	4.7	4.9	4.9	4.9	4.9
Depreciation														
Fixtures and fittings	1.0	1.0												
Vehicles	5.0	5.0	.5	.5	.5	.5	.5	.5	.5	.5	.5	.5	.5	.5
Total administration	£52.0	£64.0	5.4	5.2	5.4	5.2	5.4	5.2	5.4	5.2	5.4	5.4	5.4	5.4

ZX Ltd
Budgeted profit and loss account for the year to 31 December

Last year £		Budget £	5 Jan £	4 Feb £	4 Mar £	5 Apr £	4 May £	4 Jun £	5 Jul £	4 Aug £	4 Sep £	5 Oct £	4 Nov £	4 Dec £
370.0	Sales	450.0	18.0	22.0	26.0	60.0	40.0	36.0	30.0	28.0	28.0	60.0	80.0	22.0
28.0	Opening stock	52.0	52.0	50.2	48.0	62.4	48.2	42.4	38.9	34.3	49.7	73.2	57.0	28.4
246.0	Purchases	222.0	9.0	11.0	30.0	20.0	17.0	17.0	11.0	30.0	38.0	15.0	13.0	11.0
(52.0)	Less closing stock	(28.0)	(50.2)	(48.0)	(62.4)	(48.2)	(42.4)	(38.9)	(34.3)	(49.7)	(73.2)	(57.0)	(28.4)	(28.0)
222.0	Cost of sales	246.0	10.8	13.2	15.6	34.2	22.8	20.5	15.6	14.6	14.5	31.2	41.6	11.4
148.0 40%	Gross profit 45.3%	204.0	7.2	8.8	10.4	25.8	17.2	15.5	14.4	13.4	13.5	28.8	38.4	10.6
57.0	Factory expenses	71.0	5.9	5.9	5.9	5.9	5.9	5.9	5.9	5.9	6.0	5.9	6.0	5.9
25.0	Sales and marketing	35.0	.6	1.7	2.6	4.7	2.6	2.7	2.6	1.7	1.7	4.7	4.7	4.7
52.0	Administration	64.0	5.4	5.2	5.4	5.2	5.4	5.2	5.4	5.2	5.4	5.4	5.4	5.4
4.0	Cash discounts	5.0	.2	.2	.3	.7	.5	.4	.3	.3	.3	.7	.9	.2
138.0	Total expenses	175.0	12.1	13.0	14.5	16.5	14.4	14.2	14.2	13.1	13.4	16.7	17.0	16.2
8.0	Bank interest	6.5	.6	.6	.5	.6	.5	.5	.6	.5	.5	.6	.5	.5
2.0	Trading profit	22.5	(5.5)	(4.8)	(4.3)	8.7	2.3	.8	(.4)	(.2)	(.4)	11.5	20.9	(6.1)
—	Profit on sale of fixed assets	1.0												
£ 2.0	Net profit before tax	£ 23.5												

236

obtaining extra turnover by offering special deals to customers during such periods. If extra orders are obtainable at slack times, they can be taken at lower prices so long as this results in an additional contribution to the overheads. I discuss this topic in more detail in Chapter 17, when dealing with marginal costing.

The budgeted balance sheet

Although I have a budgeted profit and loss and cash flow, the budget is not yet complete. It is important to draw up a balance sheet as well because this shows what the working capital position will look like. The bank overdraft forecast in the cash flow is only a part of the story.

Moreover, making the balance sheet balance checks your arithmetic and highlights any errors in the figures on the other two statements.

The current year figures on the estimated balance sheet for the year just ending on page 238 become those for 'last year' on the budgeted balance sheet. The profit and loss and cash flow statements referred to below are the budgeted ones.

I start with fixed assets. A machine is to be sold for £3,500, book value £2,000, but I have to reduce the cost of plant and equipment by the original cost. I take this as £5,000. A new machine is to be bought for £10,000 so I add the net £5,000 to the existing £25,000. The cost figures for fixtures and fittings and vehicles are unchanged, there being no additions or sales.

I add the depreciation for the year shown in the budgeted profit and loss account to the accumulated depreciation for each type of asset. For plant and equipment, I deduct the accumulated figure for the machine sold. This is £3,000 (cost, £5,000, less book value, £2,000) making a net increase of £3,000. I then subtract depreciation from cost to give the net book values for each line.

I take the stock figure from the budgeted profit and loss account and the debtors from the cash flow. Payments in advance I assumed to be unchanged when I did the cash flow so this comes from the estimated balance sheet for the year just ending. The bank balance comes from the cash flow. That completes current assets and I add the figures to give the total assets.

The creditors for purchases come from the gross purchases schedule on page 214. To the figure of £20,000 at the end of December I add £6,000 for expense creditors, the same as was included in the £75,000 total last year. As explained in comment-

ZX Ltd
Budgeted balance sheet for the year to 31 December

Last year Net book value £		Cost £	Accumulated depreciation £	Budget Net book value £
	Fixed assets			
7.0	Plant and equipment	30.0	21.0	9.0
4.0	Fixtures and fittings	10.0	7.0	3.0
10.0	Vehicles	20.0	15.0	5.0
21.0		60.0	43.0	17.0
	Current assets			
52.0	Stocks			28.0
115.0	Accounts receivable (debtors)			71.0
1.0	Payments in advance			1.0
–	Cash at hand and in bank			3.0
168.0	Total current assets			103.0
189.0	**Total assets**			120.0
	Less			
	Current liabilities due within one year			
75.0	Accounts payable (creditors)			26.0
6.0	VAT payable			18.5
55.0	Bank overdraft			–
1.0	Corporation tax payable			8.0
137.0	Total current liabilities			52.5
£52.0	**Shareholders' interest in the business**			£67.5
	Represented by			
1.0	Share capital			1.0
14.0	Directors' loans			14.0
36.0	Profit and loss account balance at start of year			37.0
1.0	Profit (loss) for the year (after tax)			15.5
£52.0				£67.5

ing on the cash flow forecast, I assumed there would be no change in expense creditors.

The VAT quarterly payments schedule on page 216 showed that £33,200 would become due to Customs and Excise during the year, of which £20,700 would be paid. This means an increase in the creditors for VAT of £12,500, which I add to the previous £6,000.

There will no longer be a bank overdraft. I assume that corporation tax of £8,000 will be due on the profit – about 34 per cent.

The correct percentage figure for tax depends on the precise tax position of the company concerned. For instance, the depreciation charged in the accounts often differs from the figure allowed as a write-off of fixed assets for corporation tax. Thus, the profit for corporation tax often differs considerably from that shown in the accounts.

The £8,000 will not be paid until next year. I have already included the previous balance of £1,000 as a payment in the cash flow so the creditor was £8,000.

I add current liabilities and deduct the total from total assets to give the shareholders' interest in the business.

The share capital and the directors' loans are not expected to change so I take them from the estimated balance sheet for the year just ending. The profit and loss account balance brought forward was £37,000 as also shown on that balance sheet. The last figure to insert is the profit for the year after deducting the corporation tax mentioned above.

Now the shareholders' interest is added and I can see that my figures balance. The budgeted balance sheet highlights the dramatic reduction in both current assets and current liabilities, which will result from the better controls I intend to introduce.

The budgeted source and application of cash statement
Having completed the profit and loss, balance sheet and cash flow forecasts, I now produce the source and application of cash statement. This summarises how the improvement in the cash position will be achieved (see page 240).

The profit for the year per the profit and loss budget was £23,500. I assumed, when preparing the budgeted balance sheet, that corporation tax of £8,000 would be payable. This leaves a profit after tax of £15,500, as shown on the first line of the source and application of cash statement.

The depreciation of £12,000 is the total of the sums of £6,000 shown respectively in the detailed schedules of factory and administration expenses. I add it back to the profit and because it is not a cash payment, just a notional amount reflecting the using up of the assets.

The sale of the fixed assets would bring in £3,500. It is the cash value of the sale of the asset which affects the cash flow, not the profit.

This makes a total of £31,000 cash which will be generated by the business during the year.

ZX Ltd
Source and application of cash for year to 31 December

Source of cash		£
Profit for the year after tax		15.5
Add depreciation		12.0
Total from trading		27.5
Sale of fixed assets		3.5
Total cash available		31.0

Application of cash		
Payments not chargeable against profits		
Fixed assets bought (capital expenditure) inc VAT		11.5
Net cash left in the business		19.5
Changes in working capital		
Current assets:		
Stocks	(Increase) Decrease	24.0
Debtors	(Increase) Decrease	44.0
Payments in advance (Increase) Decrease		–
Current liabilities:		
Creditors Increase (Decrease)		(49.0)
VAT Increase (Decrease)		12.5
Tax Increase (Decrease)		7.0
Cash (used for or) released from working capital		38.5
Net increase (or decrease) during year in cash held		58.0
Opening cash balance (overdraft)		(55.0)
Closing cash balance (overdraft)		3.0

After paying for capital expenditure and tax, there will be a balance of £18,500 left in the business.

Reductions in stock and debtors will produce £68,000 but £49,000 will be used in reducing creditors. The higher creditors for VAT and tax will provide £19,500, leaving a balance released from working capital of £38,500.

Adding that to the £18,500 above gives us the net increase in cash during the year of £58,000. After deducting the overdraft, we have our closing bank balance of £3,000. Quite a transformation in the balance sheet of ZX Ltd!

So what does the ZX budget show us?

There are some important lessons in the figures. We now have a picture of the activity for the following year based on expected improvements in efficiency. It shows that the profit can be raised to a figure at which it begins to make sense. There will be a real return to the shareholder directors for their risk and effort. It also shows that this can be done while reducing the amount of cash needed to finance the business.

The budget demonstrates the importance of analysing the figures period by period. In the profit and loss account, the period results do two things. First, they provide a basis for measuring progress against target during the year. Second, they help to identify the times of the year when the business has spare capacity and when it would be worth looking for extra business at reduced profit margins.

The coming cash crisis

The analysis in the cash flow forecast is even more important because of the picture of the overdraft it gives. If the figure rose to £85,000 at the end of February without warning, the bank might well take fright. The result could be a squeeze on the liquidity of the business as the owners tried to get some money in. Done at short notice and in an unplanned way, this would probably mean taking more credit from creditors who would already be anxious about their money. Efforts to get cash in from debtors quickly would be only partially effective because of the bad habits engendered by a weak credit control system in the past.

Reducing stock levels in a hurry means stopping buying. This interferes with the reordering of materials which are being used and which are therefore most needed. An across-the-board embargo can quickly mess up production. Cutting stocks needs careful attention to the way the factory is managed, if it is to be done without practical difficulties.

In other words, good cash flow management means considered action on a planned basis. Short-term panics can only produce short-term solutions, some of which tend to aggravate the longer-term problem. The example shows the kind of situation which gets viable businesses into serious trouble, and sometimes puts them out of business, because their owners do not have the figures they need to show the bank.

The budget is a valuable management tool

The budget shows that ZX Ltd is a sound business and that its extra cash needs are short term. With that detailed cash flow forecast available, the directors can warn the bank well in advance of needing the higher overdraft. They should have no problem in getting the extra facility. The bank will see the complete picture, together with explanations as to the management action being taken to effect the promised improvements.

The figures I produced would not necessarily be the final budget. They might be fine tuned. For instance, it might be practical to delay the purchase of the new machine planned for February or to arrange to delay paying for it for a month or two, thus smoothing the overdraft peak. Such points are refinements, however. The key task of producing a budget showing a satisfactory outcome has been achieved. Now the management has some detailed targets to which to work during the year and the means of measuring its progress towards achieving them.

A summary of the key budget decisions

This summary of the key decisions taken in drawing up the ZX Ltd budget may help you to prepare one for your business. When doing so, work in the same sequence as I did. You will find that this helps you to get to the right answers without the irritating experience of having to re-do much of the arithmetic, perhaps several times. You always have to make adjustments for points overlooked or errors, especially the first time you do a budget. Alterations to one figure may affect many others. Doing it my way leaves much of the detailed adding up as long as possible, thus cutting the time needed to change a figure.

Don't treat my layouts as sacrosanct! Your budgets must suit your business and the way I have set out the figures is only an illustration. While most small businesses should find that my ideas can be readily adapted to their circumstances, you may well find that something is not quite right for you. If so, alter it.

My suggested methods and order of doing things are based on practical experience in real businesses. I have tried to explain the how and why fully, but I have not attempted to cover all the circumstances which might crop up. I have kept my example simple in order to make the principles clear. You may find one or two points not dealt with. If so, try to work out the principles involved. Common sense will usually enable you to see how to adapt my ideas and layout to your business. If you get stuck, check the other sections of the book because I have assumed that you have read and understood the earlier ones. If you are still stuck, ask your professional accountant for help.

Prepare your own budget

Profit and loss account and balance sheet for the current year
Estimate the final outcome of your figures for the current year to provide a starting point for your forecasts for next year.

Profit and loss budget
Decide on periods to use for your budget.
Decide the sales target and break this down period by period based on weekly totals.
Decide your gross profit percentage target and whether this will vary from period to period.
Calculate the cost of sales.
Enter the starting stock as already forecast for the end of the current year.
Estimate the closing stock at the end of the year.
From the above figures, work out the total purchases for the year.
Estimate the breakdown of purchases month by month.
From the above, work out the closing stock each period.
Estimate annual totals for the expenses of each department. Wages and salaries should be done in detail. So should any other major costs, like advertising, which fluctuate but, for the rest, a standard percentage increase based on inflation will be adequate, unless you know there are special reasons why they will alter. Do not spread the expenses by period at this stage.
Estimate cash discounts to customers, if applicable, in total only.
Add up total expenses.
Make the first crude estimate for bank interest payable or receivable.
Work out the annual trading profit from the above. Period figures cannot be done yet as the analysis is incomplete. If the profit looks unsatisfactory, consider how it might be improved. Your sales, gross profit and wages figures are the most likely ones to yield the required improvement. When you have an acceptable annual profit forecast, go on to the cash flow.

Cash flow forecast
On the sales schedule, work out output VAT and gross sales totals period by period. Enter the latter on the cash flow forecast.
Enter debtors at the start of the year as already forecast for the end of the current one.
Estimate debtors at the end of the year – on the basis of gross sales in closing periods and number of weeks' sales expected to be outstanding.
Enter total cash discounts from the profit and loss budget.
Work out the total cash received from debtors from the above.
Estimate total cash sales if any.
Enter fixed asset sales, including VAT if applicable, if any are known to be likely. Otherwise ignore.
Work out total cash in from the above.
Draw up the purchase payments schedule starting with the purchase figures from the profit and loss budget. Calculate the VAT and gross purchases columns. Enter the creditors at the start of the year as already forecast for the end of the current year.
Estimate the creditors at the end of the year based on the purchases for the final periods, plus VAT and the length of credit expected to be taken.
Work out on the purchase payments schedule the total payments to suppliers for the year and enter on the cash flow forecast.
Enter the total wages and salaries for the whole business – from the wages schedule prepared for the profit and loss budget.

Before entering the remaining expenses, consider whether there will be any material differences in the total of expense creditors at the end of next year from that forecast for the end of the current one. If you expect an increase, deduct it from the total expenses in the profit and loss budget. For a decrease, add it on.

Having made any such adjustment, pick out any of the expenses paid quarterly, half-yearly or annually which are large enough to be worth showing separately and enter these in the total column.

Enter the remaining monthly expenses in total in the total column by department or whatever main headings you use in the profit and loss budget. If in the latter you show each type of expense, take the total of all the monthly ones. Detailing the figures expense by expense is unnecessary. Do not spread the total across the periods at this stage. Do not include depreciation as this is not a cash item.

Work out the quarterly VAT payments from the period output and input tax figures on the sales and purchase payments schedule. Adjust for tax, if applicable, on any sales or purchases of fixed assets for which you are budgeting.

Enter the VAT in the quarters in which it will be paid. If you reclaim VAT on a monthly return, put the period figures in brackets as deductions.
Add up the total expenses.
Enter the capital expenditure planned, if any, including VAT if applicable.
Enter the provisional figure for bank interest from the profit and loss budget.
Enter expected income or corporation tax payments.
Add up the total cash out.
Enter the opening bank overdraft as forecast for the end of the current year.

Work out from the above the cash flow and the closing bank overdraft.
Sigh with relief or gasp with horror as appropriate! If with horror, review the figures to see what can be done to get to a more acceptable closing bank balance. This could include tighter financial control, postponing certain expenditure or cutting expenses. Assuming that the forecast profit is satisfactory, raising the sales estimate is unlikely to help since it will soak up more cash in working capital.

Now complete the period analysis for the cash flow budget – before that for the profit and loss, which comes last.

Enter the cash flow analysis period by period for sales including VAT.
Enter the cash discounts in proportion to sales.
Calculate the closing debtors period by period based on antici-

pated credit related to the gross sales. The last period figure must agree with the closing debtors at the end of the year, which is already in the total column.

Work out from the above the cash received from debtors period by period.
On the purchase payments schedule, work out the payments period by period after calculating the closing creditors for each period related to anticipated credit and purchases including VAT. Enter the payments to suppliers on the cash flow.

Spread the totals for wages, advertising and/or any other expenses you have decided to show separately and those for the remaining expenses period by period.

Work out from the above the total expenses and total cash out lines period by period. From these there follow the net cash flow and the closing bank balance period by period. The latter must agree with that in the total column, which you arrived at earlier.

Compare the crude forecast for bank interest, if any, with the period bank balances and adjust if necessary. Perhaps the period by period figures show that you will be able to earn interest by putting funds on deposit at certain times of the year. Both the profit and loss budget and the cash flow forecast will need amending for any change you need to make in the interest figure.

If your budget shows overdrafts in one or more periods, which exceed the facility at present agreed with your bank, consider whether you can reduce the peaks to figures within the facility by postponing expenditure to later in the year or whether there are gains in efficiency which you can make to achieve this. If not, but the budgeted profit is satisfactory and examination of the ratios of return on capital etc, explained in earlier chapters shows that the business is sound, book an appointment with your bank manager to ask for an increased facility.

Completing the profit and loss budget
Only now do you complete the period analysis for the profit

and loss budget, having reduced to a minimum the risk of having to alter all the figures because of changes to the main totals.

Enter the wages and other expense figures period by period.
Enter the cash discounts from the cash flow.
Enter the bank interest either in each period or in those in which it will be debited, whichever you prefer. A rough guess at the amounts will do.
Work out from the above the trading profit period by period.

Balance sheet and source and application of cash
Draw up these statements. The explanations given earlier are concise enough for me not to need to repeat them here.
  Now you have a budget!

Chapter 22

Practical Tips on Preparing a Budget

Budgeting can be a long, tedious task. Here are some practical points to help you avoid getting bogged down. Some are relevant even to the smallest business; others are addressed to people who work in organisations big enough to have departments and therefore need the cooperation of others in preparing the budget.

Keep it simple

The first time you write a budget, accuracy and detail are less important than getting the job done. Don't worry if you have to make some broad guesses or assumptions and skip some of the detailed steps described in the previous chapter. It is better to budget in outline than not at all. You may have to anyway to get your figures out before the start of the period to which they relate. Once it has begun, part of their value is already lost.

Keep it simple to start with. You will probably be short of time; you may not be sure of all the detailed points yourself; some of your colleagues or employees, perhaps even your superiors, may be sceptical of the value of budgets and give you grudging cooperation. It is better to build on simple foundations than risk alienating people – or getting fed up with it yourself – by demanding a mass of detail the first time. As you and your colleagues get used to budgets and learn to use them, they can be made more sophisticated. It is always quicker and easier the second time.

Involve the rest of the organisation

Try to involve your colleagues right from the start. Even if you do not expect sensible answers, do not give them the excuse that they were not asked for their views!

Unless you run your business entirely by yourself, you must

have the active cooperation of others if budgeting is to become the effective management tool it should be. You may have to win this cooperation gradually as you demonstrate its advantages.

All managerial staff should take part in preparing the budget. The more they contribute to its preparation, the more they will accept and identify with the policies and targets set. If the managing director and/or the accountant prepare the figures in isolation from other executives, it is too easy for the latter to dismiss the whole exercise as office paperwork rather than as targets for whose achievement they are responsible.

If you are the boss your prime task is to motivate your staff to work together as a team towards common objectives. People who are not so motivated tend to set personal goals for themselves which may conflict either with those of their colleagues or with the interests of the organisation as a whole. The budgeting process, when used correctly, generates discussion and exchange of ideas. It clarifies problems, improves mutual understanding and produces a group commitment to reach agreed targets. If you misuse this process, impose budgets on staff and then put on the pressure, it creates jealousy and strife. People waste energy in protecting themselves from blame for failure to achieve objectives which are not fully understood and which may well be impractical in detail or even mutually conflicting.

Surely an inaccurate budget is not very useful?

None of the advantages of budgets listed in Chapter 21 depends entirely on accuracy. All budgets are guesses about the future and the outcome is bound to be different. Obviously, the closer your guesses are the better, and it is easier to make good ones if you have detailed schedules, showing how each expense heading is made up, than if all you know is the total you spent on that item last year. It is a matter of judgement as to how much effort to put into getting that detail, especially for the first budget you do. In time your skill in guessing will improve; meanwhile differences on individual figures have a nice habit of cancelling each other out.

One of the main benefits of budgeting is that having to plan helps you to think constructively about the future of your business. You get that benefit straight away.

Look out for short cuts

It is easy to get 'lost' in a mass of detailed calculations when working out some costs. For instance, holiday pay for employees or turnover discounts to large customers are usually big figures, but the individual calculations needed to work them out in detail tend to be complicated and lengthy.

Often a quick estimate of such figures can be made. Even when the basis of this estimate is crude it may be preferable to a detailed one because of the time it saves, especially the first time you produce a budget. Reasoned estimates also have an agreeable habit of turning out right. It is amazing how close an initial quick guess often is to the figure produced after hours of careful calculations – provided you guess using sensible assumptions.

For example, to work out turnover rebates to customers in detail, customer by customer, can be tedious, especially if a sliding scale of rebate applies. If you calculate the total cost last year as a percentage of last year's sales and apply that percentage to the budgeted sales, it will save a lot of time and will probably work out right, provided your terms and the nature of your sales have not altered.

Beware also of wasting time on costs whose calculation takes much time and effort, but which turn out to be negligible in relation to other figures. An example is sundry consumable items in a factory or workshop, such as oil, grease, rags and cleaning materials. If you have not had detailed figures before, you may not know how important such expenses are. Before spending time finding out, consider whether the total is likely to be large enough to matter. Such potential time wasters are often better guessed at but this is not always obvious at first.

Are there dangers in short cuts?
Yes, but they should be apparent, given a little thought about the facts. For instance, it is tempting to take average weekly earnings of employees as a basis for estimating the wages. Such averages can be misleading if individual rates vary or if overtime or special payments are included. You will not get the right answer if you estimate the next annual pay increases on such an average. Most pay rises apply to basic pay. Though they affect social security costs, bonuses and overtime, it is not in the same ratio.

The problems about short cuts to estimating expenses in budgets is that they are not much help in controlling the business. Effective action to put right an overspend needs to be based on specific instructions to stop or delay expenditure or change the way it is incurred.

This requires an understanding of the precise nature and breakdown of costs. For example, a salesman's car expenses include:

- depreciation on car (or perhaps a leasing charge)
- tax and insurance
- accident repair bills not covered by insurance
- routine maintenance including batteries and tyres
- petrol and oil.

Only the last three costs vary with the mileage he does so only they can be reduced by management control. The first two are inevitable once the decision is made to equip the salesman with a car. If the budget is to provide effective control it must therefore separate the motor costs. If petrol prices double, it is possible to estimate quickly the effect on the organisation and consider alternatives to the present system of sales calls.

Looking at it another way, if you want to cut total motor expenses by 10 per cent without reducing the number of vehicles, you will have to lower the variable element by more than 10 per cent and you will need an analysis under the headings listed above to see by how much.

Another reason for needing detail is that, without it, an excess of actual expense over budget tends to be merely a hole in the profit. It is often difficult to find out what has caused the excess.

Therefore, the more you can analyse costs into the units which generate them, such as cars, and into headings, such as insurance and petrol, the better the planning and control process will be.

Naturally, the size of the expense must determine the time you spend on it. However, without some detail, it is difficult to manage the costs of a business properly because instructions, such as 'cut all costs by 10 per cent' or 'restrict all telephone calls', merely tend to cause short-term disruption as staff react to the latest management blitz. As soon as some other problem takes the limelight, the first is forgotten. Little permanent good results from such action but it can easily create enough temporary irritation to reduce the efficiency of the organisation. It is called 'management by crisis'. Good budgeting helps to stop it by providing the information on which to base more constructive action.

Use the same format for your budget as for your annual accounts

Budget layouts, headings and detailed schedules should be set out in the same way as your actual results; otherwise it will not be possible to compare the latter with the budget forecast. Silly though it may sound, this is a common mistake, easily made.

Salaries and wages are an example. Staff must be grouped on the wages sheets in the same way as the budget is organised, if comparable figures are to be readily available. Since there may be good reasons for the existing wages analysis, this needs attention at the budget stage, not as an afterthought.

Prepare and photocopy your layouts

You can save many hours by using copies of prepared forms. Whether you adapt the layouts used here, or you prepare your own, keep the originals blank and use photocopies of them for your workings. This way you can amend layouts readily and revise your figures with the minimum of repetitive work.

- Prepare your draft forms and photocopy them.
- Handwrite your figures on the photocopies, amending the forms as needed.
  If you need clean copies or several sets of the figures:
- Type final forms in blank.
- Copy final blank forms and type in figures on copies.
- Re-copy completed forms in the quantity needed.

Round your figures

Start with detailed figures where possible – exact pay rates, for instance, but round all totals. Totals rounded to the nearest £1,000, £100 etc, are quicker to add and easier to understand. All budgeting is estimating and it is pointless to use exact totals merely because they are the arithmetical result of your calculations, especially when they make the schedules harder to read. Be ruthless about eliminating odd pounds from all reports and principal back-up schedules.

Round the larger figures, such as sales, wages etc to the nearest £1,000, the smaller ones to the nearest £100 (£5 or £10 if the business is very small). In practice minor inaccuracies, owing to rounding, do not matter.

Keep your workings for each budget figure

Always write down and retain the basis of your estimates. Even rough workings can be invaluable later, when checking back on your figures for the reasons why actual results differ from budget.

Work in pencil

This makes it much easier to amend your figures for the inevitable changes.

VAT

Remember that any VAT you can recover is not a cost in the profit and loss budget.

Budget in accounting periods, preferably of five of four weeks

Your cash flow forecast must be broken down at least into quarters, ideally into months. Bank balances can swing in or out of credit from one month to another, particularly for a business with seasonal peaks. The balance you forecast at the end of the financial year may be no guide to the temporary finance you will need during the year.

Calendar months are not satisfactory accounting periods for most businesses, especially those, such as retailers, for whom the week is the natural measure of trade, or for those who pay much of their wages weekly rather than monthly. I suggest that you divide the year into 12 periods, 4 of five weeks and 8 of four weeks or 13 four-week ones if you prefer them to be the same length.

Efficient accounting is easier with periods because:

1. The period always ends on the same day of the week, usually

(though not necessarily) at the weekend. Accounting routines then cause the minimum disruption. For instance, production programmes etc tend to finish at weekends and stocktaking causes less disruption than if done in the middle of the week.

2. People soon get used to the end of the period being every fifth or fourth week. They tend to remember the need for routine reports and the necessary accounting work goes more smoothly as a consequence.

3. Periods are easier to compare being in five or four weeks rather than irregular numbers of calendar trading days. With 12 periods, the dates are always within a day or two of the end of the calendar month – especially if you do not work at weekends.

4. Using 12 periods also allows you to begin each quarter with a five-week period giving yourself the maximum time for quarterly accounts, if you produce these. I therefore prefer 12 periods to 13 of four weeks.

When should I budget?

The budget should be completed before the start of the financial year. This is the time to plan. Accounts staff are busy on the annual accounts immediately after the new year begins; moreover planning should be at least 12 months ahead.

Do not change your budget during the year

I do not believe in changing a *budget* just because some of the circumstances have altered. I prefer to continue to report against the original budget and to make instead a revised *forecast*.

Once you know what profit will result from the figures in the budget, it is usually easy to work out the effect of differences as events progress. You will find that only a few figures are important enough for changes to matter, so you can readily produce updated *forecasts* of your likely profit whenever you wish as the year goes on. These are quicker to do, because they need only show the main totals and are thus a much more flexible way of predicting the outcome than revising the budget.

Some things you can do in advance

You will find it much easier to get your budget done on time if you organise your records in advance to produce the basic facts you will need.

Many of the figures you will have to forecast are easy. Some are known, like rent fixed under a lease, or are bills, such as rates or insurance, for which you can estimate the percentage increase without any error mattering much. Other costs, such as telephone, postage or stationery, may be less predictable but are small enough in most businesses for a guess based on last year to be accurate enough.

It is usually just a few figures which take most time to work out and are big enough for changes in them to make an impact on the profit. If the estimates for these are not based on detailed schedules you will not be able to see the reason for variations from your budget. It is often possible to sort out much of the detail you need in advance.

If you are doing a budget for a business you haven't yet started, you will not be able to detail everything because you will not have much to go on. Even so, you should be able to break some headings down on the basis of what you do know.

Motor expenses are an example. To plan at all, you must have some idea of how many vehicles you will need and what types. I explained earlier why it is helpful to divide this expense into its different elements, such as licences, insurance, repairs, fuel etc, as they change by different amounts and for different reasons. If you leave this until you begin your budget, sorting out the figures will take time you have not got.

If you are already in business, you can organise your existing records to give you the details. How you arrange this depends on your accounting system, but it is usually not difficult either to build up separate totals or mark the entries in some way in order to identify the different elements.

Getting organised

1. Get your budget schedules ready in blank as explained on page 252. As far as possible, use the same layouts and headings as for your annual accounts but with 13 columns – 12 months plus annual total – as illustrated in the examples in earlier chapters.

2. Estimate your current year's results in the 'last year' column.
3. Sort out the detailed information needed for the key figures.

Estimating the current year's results

'Last year' is the year either nearly over or just finished. 'Budget' is the new one for which you are budgeting.

Last year's results are the starting point for the budget. If you are budgeting before the current year ends, as you should be, you will have to estimate your sales and expenses for the last month or two.

If you do have quarterly or half-yearly accounts for your business, you may lack detailed information on some expenses for the current year. However, even elementary records will tell you your sales figures and your wage costs and you have invoices for your major expenses. You therefore know your actual results for the year to date and can add an estimate of the figures for the remainder of it. Your gross profit percentage is probably the biggest uncertainty but past results and your knowledge of the present should enable you to make a sensible guess.

Thus, for each heading in your budget you will need to estimate the total for the current year before you can budget for the next year. When the budget is complete, you will have a forecast for the present year nearly finished as well as for the next year not yet begun.

Do not wait until after the present year has ended to get the actual figures for a full year. Apart from having to cope with finishing writing up your records, to produce the annual figures, and the budget at the same time, you will lose the benefits of budgeting for the first month or two of the next year.

The detailed schedules you may need

Here are some ideas of what detailed schedules you may need to prepare your budget. Many of them can be started well ahead and gradually filled in, thus reducing the last-minute rush.

The sales budget
How this is prepared depends on the nature of your business.

Some of the questions you may need to answer to base your forecast on a logical framework are:

Do you need figures

in money only or in units such as quantities of product or hours of time as well?
broken down by product, branch, department, sales area or country?

What are expected selling prices for

existing products?
new products or revised specifications?
special offers?
bulk sales or quantity discounts?
surplus stock sell-off?
exports?

Will there be any price increases during the year?

Do you give discounts for

prompt payment?
volume rebates?

Other factors you may wish to consider are as follows.

State of the market
Is it growing, static or declining, either nationally or in your area? How important to your business are general economic trends? Will changes in social habits and tastes, such as growth in convenience foods, or the decline in cinema attendances, have any impact on your market? Will it be affected by demands for higher standards on, say, noise and pollution or laws such as the Health and Safety at Work Act?

Product changes
Do you have plans for improvements to existing products or services or for introducing new ones? Will you obtain more business by extending your premises, adding more staff or new equipment?

The competition
This means not only your local competitors in the same trade but also the national supply/demand situation. Petrol and calculators are examples of products which have been the subject

of intense price competition because manufacturers' production capacity greatly exceeded demand.

Have you thought about what changes in your market may be about to occur? Some examples of changes which have caught people out in the past are self-service, supermarkets, launderettes, transistors, electronic circuits in hi-fi equipment and digital watches. All these caused revolutions in their various industries, created upheavals in established businesses and put some out of business. Yet none of them happened overnight!

All new ideas and technologies are written up both in the national and in the trade press long before they make their main impact. It takes time for volume production to build up, new ideas to be accepted, new markets created; plenty of time for the businessperson to take notice and plan accordingly.

It seems that many heads of businesses, both large and small, do too little reading, are not aware of the wider world in which they operate and are caught out by changes which they should have spotted in time. Are you doing enough to ensure that it does not happen to you? Everyone tends to be enveloped in their own small world. What positive steps are you taking to widen yours?

What sales data do you have?
A new business has special problems in guessing its sales figures. However, you should not be in business if you do not have some targets, do not at least know how much you need to sell to cover your costs and how this compares, either with your competitors, with a typical business of your kind, or with the size of your market. So why not budget on that basis?

An existing business can start with last year's figures and add something for inflation. But can you not be a little more sophisticated? How do your activities break down'

- into product groups at similar profit margins?
- into single products (or services)?
- by department?
- by separate shop, warehouse, factory etc?

The more you can analyse your totals into the constituent items or services you sell, the sounder will be the basis of your estimates and the more help they will be in running the business.

If you sell time see Chapter 16, Pricing Your Time. The section

'Understand your costs and make better business decisions' may also help you to organise your budget.

Staff costs
In a business which is large enough to be divided into departments, this is not a heading which appears as such in the accounts or the budget. However, it is useful to highlight your total costs of employing staff by putting all the wages and salaries department by department and person by person on one schedule for the entire business. This helps to ensure that no one is overlooked. The totals for each department are then distributed under the relevant headings as used in the accounts.

Depending upon your business, you may need to consider:

- expected changes in your staff
- pay increases and on what dates
- overtime
- bonuses
- extra payments such as dirty money
- holiday pay
- pensions.

Having worked out their pay, what about the other costs which staff generate? If you plan to recruit new people, do not forget extras which may be shown under different headings; for example, motor expenses for any vehicles the newcomers will need. Other possibilities are:

- travel and subsistence expenses
- training
- recruitment costs
- protective clothing.

Marketing and sales costs
These vary with each business but often include:

- advertising in the press or on TV
- other promotional costs, such as trade exhibitions
- sales aids, such as merchandisers, leaflets and showcards.

Factory, shop or office costs
These are usually the easier ones to estimate. Some which may need a little thought are:

- repairs and maintenance: buildings equipment
- utility costs: electricity, gas and telephone
- heating fuel: oil or coal
- moulds, special tools and jigs, external testing fees or design and artwork for packaging. (These can be substantial when one launches a new product.)

Capital expenditure
What will you need to spend on:

- buildings?
- factory, laboratory, shop and office equipment?
- vehicles, sales or management?

Naturally, this checklist mentions only a few of the many costs which apply to different businesses. Some may not apply or be insignificant in your business; you may have others to add.

Remember, your first budget will not – cannot – cover all this in detail. You are most unlikely to have the time or sufficient understanding of the facts. So, first time round, you will have to cut some corners, especially if your executives either lack experience or are not fully converted to the idea of budgets.